Slow Cooker
Recipes

Publications International, Ltd.

Favorite Brand Name Recipes at www.fbnr.com

© 2008 Publications International, Ltd.
Recipes, text and photography © 2008 Campbell Soup Company

Campbell's®, Pace®, Prego®, V8® and Swanson® are registered trademarks of CSC Brands LP. All rights reserved.
Pepperidge Farm® is a registered trademark of Pepperidge Farm, Incorporated. All rights reserved.

Copyrights and trademarks are used by Publications International, Ltd. with permission.

Louis Weber, CEO
Publications International, Ltd.
7373 North Cicero Avenue
Lincolnwood, IL 60712

Permission is never granted for commercial purposes.

Special thanks to the Campbell's Kitchen, Lucinda Ayers, Vice President, and Catherine Marschean-Spivak, Group Manager.

Photography on pages 9, 11, 13, 39, 41, 43, 45, 47, 71, 73, 75, 77, 79, 81, 83, 85, 87, 89, 99, 101, 103, 105, 107, 109, 111, 113, 115, 117, 133, 135, 137, 139, 141, 143, 145, 147 and 149 by Stephen Hamilton Photographics, Inc., Chicago.

Photographers: Raymond Barrera, Tate Hunt, Brian Wetzstein
Photographers' Assistant: Chris Gurley
Prop Stylist: Tom Hamilton
Food Stylists: Kim Hartman, David Kennedy, Walter Moeller
Assistant Food Stylists: Lissa Levy, Breana Moeller

Pictured on front cover: Savory Pot Roast *(page 6)*.

Pictured on back cover (clockwise from top): Albondigas Soup *(page 40)*, Sweet 'n' Spicy Barbecued Brisket *(page 95)* and Chicken in Creamy Sun-Dried Tomato Sauce *(page 18)*.

ISBN 13: 978-1-4127-2870-6
ISBN 10: 1-4127-2870-3

Library of Congress Control Number: 2008920458

Manufactured in China.

8 7 6 5 4 3 2 1

Microwave Cooking: Microwave ovens vary in wattage. Use the cooking times as guidelines and check for doneness before adding more time.

Preparation/Cooking Times: Preparation times are based on the approximate amount of time required to assemble the recipe before cooking, baking, chilling or serving. These times include preparation steps such as measuring, chopping and mixing. The fact that some preparations and cooking can be done simultaneously is taken into account. Preparation of optional ingredients and serving suggestions is not included.

Contents

Welcome to Slow Cooking!

Slow cookers continue to be popular because they help you save time and there is easy cleanup. They also let you put together ingredients early in the day and come home to a hot, delicious wholesome meal. Inside you'll find main dishes, all-in-one meals, hearty soups and stews, potluck and party recipes, internationally-inspired favorites and even some easy-to-prepare desserts.

Here are a few things to remember as you break out your slow cooker:

■ For easy cleanup, spray the crock with nonstick cooking spray before adding the food. Or, try the new slow cooker liner bags. (To clean your slow cooker, follow the manufacturer's instructions.)

■ Slow cookers cook best when they're two-thirds to three-quarters full. That's because most slow cookers' heating units are coiled inside the outer walls that surround the crockery insert rather than on the bottom of the crock.

■ Keep a lid on it! The slow cooker can take as long as 20 minutes to regain the heat lost when the cover is removed.

If the recipe calls for stirring or checking the dish near the end of the cooking time, replace the lid as quickly as you can.

Adapting Recipes

If you'd like to adapt your favorite recipe to a slow cooker, find a similar slow cooker recipe. Note the cooking time and temperature, the amount of liquid, the quantity of meat and vegetables and how they're cut. Also note in what order the ingredients are added to the cooker. (Firmer vegetables, such as potatoes and carrots, sometimes go into the bottom of the cooker.) Because the slow cooker retains moisture, you may have to reduce the amount of liquid in a non-slow-cooker recipe by as much as half. Slow cooking tends to enhance the flavors of whole or fresh herbs, so use only about half the amount called for in the recipe. Add fresh herbs during the last half hour of cooking. Add dairy products at the end of cooking time so they do not curdle.

Selecting the Right Meat

Slow cookers are perfect for less-tender cuts of meat, which come out fork-tender and flavorful in a slow cooker. So save some money and pick the cheaper, less-tender cuts such as round steak, chuck roast, lamb shanks, stew meats and others that require long cooking times with other cooking methods.

Preparing Vegetables

Pay careful attention to the recipe instructions so you're sure to cut vegetables in the proper size and add them to the slow cooker in the correct order. Frozen vegetables should be thawed before adding to the slow cooker. Frozen foods lower the temperature inside the cooker and can play havoc with cooking times if not thawed first.

Reducing Fat

Slow cooking can be reduced-fat cooking. First, less-expensive cuts of meat that are perfect for the slow cooker are lower in fat than other cuts. When using fatty meats, try browning them first in a skillet on the stovetop to cook away some of the fat before cooking in the slow cooker.

Secondly, since slow cookers retain moisture, you don't have to begin with as much fat. Actually, much of the time, you don't have to begin with any fat. Any flavorful liquid, such as Swanson® Broth, Campbell's® Soup, or Pace® Salsa or Picante Sauce, can stand in for fat and become an excellent sauce or gravy for the recipe.

Food Safety Tips

If you do any advance preparation, such as trimming meat or cutting vegetables, make sure you keep the food covered and refrigerated until you're ready to add it to the cooker. Store uncooked meats and vegetables separately. After you've prepared raw meat, poultry or fish, remember to wash your cutting board, utensils, countertops, sink and hands with hot soapy water. (Many cooks have plastic cutting boards that they use just for meat preparation so they can wash and sterilize them in the dishwasher after use.)

Once your dish is cooked, serve it immediately. After serving, transfer food to a clean container, cover and refrigerate it immediately. Do not reheat leftovers in the slow cooker. Use a microwave oven, the range-top or the oven for reheating in a suitable container.

Enjoy slow-cooking for its great taste and satisfying meals, ease of preparation and the time saved for other pleasant activities!

5

Main-Dish Meals

Savory Pot Roast

MAKES 8 SERVINGS

PREP
10 MINUTES

COOK
8 TO 9 HOURS

1 can (10¾ ounces) Campbell's® Condensed Cream of Mushroom Soup (Regular, 98% Fat Free **or** 25% Less Sodium)

1 pouch (1 ounce) Campbell's® Dry Onion Soup & Recipe Mix

6 medium potatoes, cut into quarters (about 6 cups)

6 medium carrots, cut into 2-inch pieces (about 3 cups)

3½- to 4-pound boneless beef bottom round roast **or** chuck pot roast

1. Stir the mushroom soup, onion soup mix, potatoes and carrots in a 3½-quart slow cooker. Add the beef and turn to coat.

2. Cover and cook on LOW for 8 to 9 hours* or until the beef is fork-tender.

Or on HIGH for 4 to 5 hours.

Chicken & Bean Burritos

MAKES 12 BURRITOS

PREP
10 MINUTES

COOK
6 TO 7 HOURS

1 can (10¾ ounces) Campbell's® Condensed
Cheddar Cheese Soup

1 teaspoon garlic powder

2 tablespoons chili powder

2 pounds skinless, boneless chicken thighs, cut
into 1-inch pieces

1 can (about 14 ounces) black beans, rinsed and
drained

1 can (about 14 ounces) pinto beans, rinsed and
drained

12 flour tortillas (8- to 10-inch), warmed
Chopped lettuce
Chopped tomato

1. Stir the soup, garlic powder, chili powder and chicken in
a 3½- to 4-quart slow cooker.

2. Cover and cook on LOW for 6 to 7 hours* or until the
chicken is cooked through.

3. Mash the black and pinto beans with a fork in a medium
bowl. Stir into the chicken mixture. Spoon **about ½ cup** of
the chicken mixture down the center of **each** tortilla. Top
with the lettuce and tomato. Fold the tortillas around the
filling.

Or on HIGH for 3 to 4 hours.

Creamy Beef Stroganoff

MAKES 9 SERVINGS

PREP
15 MINUTES

COOK
8 TO 9 HOURS

2 cans (10¾ ounces **each**) Campbell's® Condensed Cream of Mushroom Soup (Regular, 98% Fat Free **or** 25% Less Sodium)

¼ cup water

2 tablespoons Worcestershire sauce

1 package (8 ounces) sliced white mushrooms

3 medium onions, coarsely chopped (about 1½ cups)

3 cloves garlic, minced

½ teaspoon ground black pepper

2 pounds boneless beef bottom round steak, sliced diagonally into strips

1 cup sour cream

Hot cooked egg noodles

Chopped fresh parsley (optional)

Campbell's Kitchen Tip

For more overall flavor and color, brown the beef before adding it to the slow cooker.

1. Stir the soup, water, Worcestershire sauce, mushrooms, onions, garlic and black pepper in a 6-quart slow cooker. Add the beef and stir to coat.

2. Cover and cook on LOW for 8 to 9 hours* or until the beef is cooked through.

3. Stir the sour cream into the cooker. Serve with the egg noodles. Top with the parsley, if desired.

Or on HIGH for 4 to 5 hours.

Curried Turkey Cutlets

MAKES 8 SERVINGS

PREP
10 MINUTES

COOK
6 TO 7 HOURS

2 cans (10¾ ounces **each**) Campbell's® Condensed Cream of Chicken Soup (Regular **or** 98% Fat Free)

2 tablespoons water

1 tablespoon curry powder

½ teaspoon cracked black pepper

8 turkey breast cutlets (about 2 pounds)

¼ cup heavy cream

½ cup seedless red grapes, cut in half

Hot cooked rice **or** seasoned rice blend

Campbell's Kitchen Tip

This recipe is delicious served with any of these toppers: chutney, toasted coconut, sliced almonds **and/or** raisins.

1. Stir the soup, water, curry powder and black pepper in a 3½- to 4-quart slow cooker. Add the turkey and turn to coat.

2. Cover and cook on LOW for 6 to 7 hours* or until the turkey is cooked through.

3. Stir the cream and grapes into the cooker. Serve with the rice.

*Or on HIGH for 3 to 4 hours.

Balsamic Beef with Mushrooms

MAKES 6 SERVINGS

PREP
15 MINUTES

COOK
7 TO 8 HOURS

Vegetable cooking spray

2 pounds boneless beef chuck roast, 1 inch thick

2⅔ cups Prego® Traditional Italian Sauce

⅓ cup balsamic vinegar

2 packages (8 ounces **each**) sliced mushrooms

1 slice bacon, cooked and crumbled

Hot cooked egg noodles

1. Spray a 10-inch skillet with the cooking spray. Heat over medium-high heat for 1 minute. Add the beef. Cook for 6 minutes, turning it halfway through cooking.

2. Stir the sauce, vinegar, mushrooms and bacon in a 5-quart slow cooker. Add the beef and turn to coat.

3. Cover and cook on LOW for 7 to 8 hours* or until the beef is fork-tender. Serve with the egg noodles.

Or on HIGH for 4 to 5 hours.

Chicken & Herb Dumplings

MAKES 8 SERVINGS

PREP
20 MINUTES

COOK
7 TO 8 HOURS,
45 MINUTES

2 pounds skinless, boneless chicken breasts **and/or** thighs, cut into 1-inch pieces

5 medium carrots, cut into 1-inch pieces (about 2½ cups)

4 stalks celery, cut into 1-inch pieces (about 2 cups)

2 cups frozen whole kernel corn

3½ cups Swanson® Chicken Broth (Regular, Natural Goodness™ **or** Certified Organic)

¼ teaspoon ground black pepper

¼ cup all-purpose flour

½ cup water

2 cups all-purpose baking mix

⅔ cup milk

1 tablespoon chopped fresh rosemary leaves **or** 1 teaspoon dried rosemary leaves, crushed

Campbell's Kitchen Tip

Leaving the lid slightly ajar while cooking the dumplings prevents condensation from dripping onto the food.

1. Stir the chicken, carrots, celery, corn, broth and black pepper in a 6-quart slow cooker.

2. Cover and cook on LOW for 7 to 8 hours* or until the chicken is cooked through.

3. Stir the flour and water in a small bowl. Stir into the cooker. Turn the heat to HIGH. Cover and cook for 5 minutes or until the mixture boils and thickens.

4. Stir the baking mix, milk and rosemary in a medium bowl. Drop the batter by rounded tablespoonfuls over the chicken mixture. Tilt the lid to vent and cook on HIGH for 40 minutes or until the dumplings are cooked in the center.

Or on HIGH for 4 to 5 hours.

Chicken in Creamy Sun-Dried Tomato Sauce

MAKES 8 SERVINGS

PREP
15 MINUTES

COOK
7 TO 8 HOURS

2 cans (10¾ ounces **each**) Campbell's® Condensed Cream of Chicken with Herbs Soup

1 cup Chablis **or** other dry white wine*

¼ cup coarsely chopped pitted kalamata **or** oil-cured olives

2 tablespoons drained capers

2 cloves garlic, minced

1 can (14 ounces) artichoke hearts, drained and chopped

1 cup drained, coarsely chopped sun-dried tomatoes

8 skinless, boneless chicken breast halves (about 2 pounds)

½ cup chopped fresh basil leaves (optional)

Hot cooked rice, egg noodles **or** mashed potatoes

1. Stir the soup, wine, olives, capers, garlic, artichokes and tomatoes in a 3½-quart slow cooker. Add the chicken and turn to coat.

2. Cover and cook on LOW for 7 to 8 hours** or until the chicken is cooked through. Sprinkle with the basil, if desired. Serve with the rice, noodles or potatoes.

*You can substitute Swanson® Chicken Broth for the wine, if desired.

**Or on HIGH for 4 to 5 hours.

Creamy Blush Sauce with Turkey & Penne

MAKES 8 SERVINGS

PREP
10 MINUTES

COOK
7 TO 8 HOURS

STAND
10 MINUTES

Easy Substitution Tip

You can substitute 8 bone-in chicken thighs (about 2 pounds) for the turkey thighs. Makes 6 servings.

4 turkey thighs, skin removed (about 3 pounds)

1 jar (1 pound 9.75 ounces) Prego® Chunky Garden Mushroom & Green Pepper Italian Sauce

½ teaspoon crushed red pepper (optional)

½ cup half-and-half

Hot cooked penne pasta

Grated Parmesan cheese

1. Place the turkey into a 3½- to 5-quart slow cooker. Pour the sauce over the turkey and sprinkle with the red pepper.

2. Cover and cook on LOW for 7 to 8 hours* or until the turkey is cooked through. Remove the turkey from the cooker to a cutting board. Let stand for 10 minutes. Remove the turkey meat from the bones.

3. Stir the turkey meat and the half-and-half into the cooker. Spoon the turkey mixture over the pasta. Sprinkle with the cheese.

Or on HIGH for 4 to 5 hours.

Orange Chicken with Green Onions and Walnuts

MAKES 8 SERVINGS

PREP
10 MINUTES

COOK
8 TO 9 HOURS

1½ cups Swanson® Chicken Broth (Regular, Natural Goodness™ **or** Certified Organic)

¼ cup teriyaki sauce

3 cloves garlic, minced

¾ cup orange marmalade

4 green onions, sliced (about ½ cup)

2 tablespoons cornstarch

8 chicken thighs, skin removed (about 2 pounds)

½ cup walnut pieces

Hot cooked rice

1. Stir the broth, teriyaki sauce, garlic, marmalade, ¼ **cup** green onions and cornstarch in a 6-quart slow cooker. Add the chicken and turn to coat.

2. Cover and cook on LOW for 8 to 9 hours* or until the chicken is cooked through. Sprinkle with the walnuts and remaining green onions. Serve with the rice.

Or on HIGH for 4 to 5 hours.

Hearty Mixed Bean Stew with Sausage

MAKES 8 SERVINGS

PREP
15 MINUTES

COOK
7 TO 8 HOURS

¾ pound sweet Italian pork sausage, casing removed

10 cups Swanson® Chicken Broth (Regular, Natural Goodness™ **or** Certified Organic)

¼ teaspoon ground black pepper

2 medium carrots, chopped (about ⅔ cup)

1 stalk celery, chopped (about ½ cup)

4 ounces dried pinto beans (about ¾ cup)

4 ounces dried navy beans (about ¾ cup)

4 ounces dried kidney beans (about ¾ cup)

6 sun-dried tomatoes in oil, drained and thinly sliced (about ¼ cup)

Grated Parmesan cheese

1. Cook the sausage in a 10-inch skillet over medium-high heat until it's well browned, stirring frequently to separate meat. Pour off fat.

2. Stir the sausage, broth, black pepper, carrots, celery and beans in a 5-quart slow cooker.

3. Cover and cook on LOW for 7 to 8 hours*.

4. Stir in the tomatoes. Cover and cook for 1 hour or until the beans are tender. Sprinkle with the cheese.

Or on HIGH for 4 to 4½ hours.

Ratatouille with Penne

MAKES 4 SERVINGS

PREP
15 MINUTES

COOK
5½ TO 6 HOURS

1 can (10¾ ounces) Campbell's® Condensed Tomato Soup

1 tablespoon olive oil

⅛ teaspoon ground black pepper

1 small eggplant, peeled and cut into ½-inch cubes (about 5 cups)

1 medium zucchini, thinly sliced (about 1½ cups)

1 medium red pepper, diced (about 1 cup)

1 large onion, sliced (about 1 cup)

1 clove garlic, minced

Hot cooked penne pasta

Grated Parmesan cheese (optional)

1. Stir the soup, olive oil, black pepper, eggplant, zucchini, red pepper, onion and garlic in a 4- to 5½-quart slow cooker.

2. Cover and cook on LOW for 5½ to 6 hours* or until the vegetables are tender.

3. Serve over the pasta. Sprinkle with the cheese, if desired.

Or on HIGH for 2½ to 3 hours.

Coq Au Vin

MAKES 6 SERVINGS

PREP
10 MINUTES

COOK
8 TO 9 HOURS

1 package (10 ounces) sliced mushrooms

1 bag (16 ounces) frozen whole small white onions, thawed

1 sprig fresh rosemary leaves

2 pounds skinless, boneless chicken thighs **and/or** breasts, cut into 1-inch strips

¼ cup cornstarch

1 can (10¾ ounces) Campbell's® Condensed Golden Mushroom Soup

1 cup Burgundy **or** other dry red wine

Hot mashed **or** oven-roasted potatoes

1. Place the mushrooms, onions, rosemary and chicken into a 3½-quart slow cooker.

2. Stir the cornstarch, soup and wine in a small bowl. Pour over the chicken and vegetables.

3. Cover and cook on LOW for 8 to 9 hours*. Remove the rosemary. Serve with the mashed potatoes.

Or on HIGH for 4 to 5 hours.

Creamy Chicken & Wild Rice

MAKES 8 SERVINGS

PREP
10 MINUTES

COOK
7 TO 8 HOURS

2 cans (10¾ ounces **each**) Campbell's® Condensed Cream of Chicken Soup (Regular **or** 98% Fat Free)

1½ cups water

4 large carrots, thickly sliced (about 3 cups)

1 package (6 ounces) **uncooked** seasoned long-grain and wild rice mix

8 skinless, boneless chicken breast halves (about 2 pounds)

1. Stir the soup, water, carrots, rice and seasoning packet in a 3½-quart slow cooker. Add the chicken and turn to coat.

2. Cover and cook on LOW for 7 to 8 hours* or until the chicken is cooked through.

Or on HIGH for 4 to 5 hours.

Herbed Turkey Breast

MAKES 8 SERVINGS

1 can (10¾ ounces) Campbell's® Condensed Cream of Mushroom Soup (Regular, 98% Fat Free **or** 25% Less Sodium)

½ cup water

4½- to 5-pound turkey breast

1 teaspoon poultry seasoning

1 tablespoon chopped fresh parsley

Hot mashed potatoes

PREP
10 MINUTES

COOK
8 TO 9 HOURS

STAND
10 MINUTES

1. Stir the soup and water in a 3½- to 6-quart slow cooker. Rinse the turkey with cold water and pat it dry. Rub the turkey with the poultry seasoning and place in the cooker. Sprinkle with the parsley.

2. Cover and cook on LOW for 8 to 9 hours* or until the turkey is cooked through. Let the turkey stand for 10 minutes before slicing. Serve with the mashed potatoes.

Or on HIGH for 4 to 5 hours.

Campbell's Kitchen Tip

If using a frozen turkey breast, thaw before cooking.

Golden Mushroom Pork & Apples

MAKES 8 SERVINGS

PREP
10 MINUTES

COOK
8 TO 9 HOURS

2 cans (10¾ ounces **each**) Campbell's® Condensed Golden Mushroom Soup

½ cup water

1 tablespoon packed brown sugar

1 tablespoon Worcestershire sauce

1 teaspoon dried thyme leaves, crushed

8 boneless pork chops, ¾ inch thick (about 2 pounds)

4 large Granny Smith apples, sliced

2 large onions, sliced (about 2 cups)

1. Stir the soup, water, brown sugar, Worcestershire and thyme in a 3½-quart slow cooker. Add the pork, apples and onions.

2. Cover and cook on LOW for 8 to 9 hours* or until the pork is cooked through.

Or on HIGH for 4 to 5 hours.

Autumn Beef Pot Roast Au Jus

MAKES 6 SERVINGS

1 can (10½ ounces) Campbell's® Condensed Beef Broth

2 teaspoons dried thyme leaves, crushed

1½ pounds sweet potatoes, peeled and cut into 1-inch chunks (about 4 cups)*

2 medium Granny Smith apples, cored and cut into wedges

1 medium onion, coarsely chopped (about ½ cup)

2-pound boneless beef chuck pot roast

PREP
15 MINUTES

COOK
10 TO 12 HOURS

1. Stir the broth, thyme, sweet potatoes, apples and onion in a 3½-quart slow cooker. Add the beef and turn to coat.

2. Cover and cook on LOW for 10 to 12 hours** or until the beef is fork-tender.

*Or use a combination of red-skinned potatoes and peeled sweet potatoes, cut into 1-inch chunks.

**Or on HIGH for 5 to 6 hours.

Braised Short Ribs with Red Wine Tomato Sauce

MAKES 8 SERVINGS

PREP
10 MINUTES

COOK
7 TO 8 HOURS

4 pounds beef short ribs, cut into serving-sized pieces

$2\frac{2}{3}$ cups Prego® Fresh Mushroom Italian Sauce

1 cup dry red wine

1 bag (16 ounces) fresh **or** frozen whole baby carrots

1 large onion, chopped (about 1 cup)

Hot cooked rice

1. Season the ribs as desired.

2. Stir the sauce, wine, carrots and onion in a $3\frac{1}{2}$-quart slow cooker. Add the ribs and turn to coat.

3. Cover and cook on LOW for 7 to 8 hours* or until the ribs are fork-tender. Serve with the rice.

Or on HIGH for 4 to 5 hours.

Sausage & Brown Rice Dinner

MAKES 9 SERVINGS

1 can (10¾ ounces) Campbell's® Condensed Cream of Mushroom Soup (Regular, 98% Fat Free **or** 25% Less Sodium)

1 can (10½ ounces) Campbell's® Condensed Chicken Broth

1¼ cups water

1 cup **uncooked** regular brown rice

1 large red pepper, chopped (about 1 cup)

1 medium onion, chopped (about ½ cup)

3 cloves garlic, minced

1 teaspoon dried thyme leaves, crushed

2 pounds sweet Italian pork sausage, cut into 1½-inch pieces

PREP
15 MINUTES

COOK
7 TO 8 HOURS

1. Stir the soup, broth, water, rice, pepper, onion, garlic, thyme and sausage in a 6-quart slow cooker.

2. Cover and cook on LOW for 7 to 8 hours* or until the sausage is cooked through.

Or on HIGH for 4 to 5 hours.

Campbell's Kitchen Tip

For more overall flavor and color, brown the sausage before adding it to the slow cooker.

Golden Chicken with Noodles

MAKES 8 SERVINGS

PREP
5 MINUTES

COOK
7 TO 8 HOURS

2 cans (10¾ ounces **each**) Campbell's® Condensed Cream of Chicken Soup (Regular **or** 98% Fat Free)

½ cup water

¼ cup lemon juice

1 tablespoon Dijon-style mustard

1½ teaspoons garlic powder

8 large carrots, thickly sliced (about 6 cups)

8 skinless, boneless chicken breast halves (about 2 pounds)

4 cups hot cooked egg noodles

Chopped fresh parsley

1. Stir the soup, water, lemon juice, mustard, garlic powder and carrots in a 3½-quart slow cooker. Add the chicken and turn to coat.

2. Cover and cook on LOW for 7 to 8 hours* or until the chicken is cooked through. Serve with the noodles. Sprinkle with the parsley.

Or on HIGH for 4 to 5 hours.

Ham & Scalloped Potato Casserole

MAKES 8 SERVINGS

Vegetable cooking spray

1 pound diced cooked ham (about 2 cups)

4 pounds potatoes, peeled and thinly sliced (about 8 cups)

1 large onion, sliced (about 1 cup)

2 cans (10¾ ounces **each**) Campbell's® Condensed Cheddar Cheese Soup

1 cup milk

1 teaspoon paprika

PREP
25 MINUTES

COOK
7 TO 8 HOURS

1. Spray the inside of a 5- to 6-quart slow cooker with the cooking spray. Layer the ham, potatoes and onion in the cooker.

2. Mix the soup and milk in a small bowl. Pour over the potato mixture. Sprinkle with the paprika.

3. Cover and cook on LOW for 7 to 8 hours* or until the potatoes are tender.

Or on HIGH for 4 to 5 hours.

Soups, Chilis & Stews

Lentil Soup with Beef

MAKES 8 SERVINGS

PREP
15 MINUTES

COOK
7 TO 8 HOURS

3 cans (10½ ounces **each**) Campbell's® Condensed French Onion Soup

1 soup can water

3 stalks celery, sliced (about 1½ cups)

3 large carrots, sliced (about 1½ cups)

1½ cups dried lentils

1 can (about 14½ ounces) diced tomatoes

1 teaspoon dried thyme leaves, crushed

3 cloves garlic, minced

2 pounds beef for stew, cut into 1-inch pieces

1. Stir the soup, water, celery, carrots, lentils, tomatoes, thyme, garlic and beef in a 4½- to 5-quart slow cooker. Season as desired.

2. Cover and cook on LOW for 7 to 8 hours* or until the beef is fork-tender.

Or on HIGH for 4 to 5 hours.

Albondigas Soup

MAKES 6 SERVINGS

PREP
15 MINUTES

COOK
7 TO 8 HOURS

4 cups Swanson® Beef Broth (Regular, 50% Less Sodium **or** Certified Organic)*

1 jar (11 ounces) Pace® Thick & Chunky Salsa

1 can (about 14½ ounces) diced tomatoes

3 cloves garlic, minced

¾ cup **uncooked** regular long-grain white rice
   Mexican Meatballs

3 tablespoons chopped fresh cilantro leaves

1. Stir the broth, salsa, tomatoes, garlic, rice and *Mexican Meatballs* in a 6-quart slow cooker.

2. Cover and cook on LOW for 7 to 8 hours** or until the rice is tender and the meatballs are cooked through. Sprinkle with the cilantro before serving.

Mexican Meatballs: Mix thoroughly **1 pound** of ground beef, **1** egg, ⅓ **cup** cornmeal, ⅓ **cup** water, **1 teaspoon** hot pepper sauce and **3 tablespoons** chopped fresh cilantro leaves in a large bowl. Shape the beef mixture **firmly** into **24** meatballs. Add to the cooker as directed above.

*This recipe is also delicious with Swanson® Chicken Broth (Regular, Natural Goodness™ **or** Certified Organic) instead of the beef broth.*

***Or on HIGH for 4 to 5 hours.*

Chicken Gumbo Ya Ya

MAKES 8 SERVINGS

PREP
20 MINUTES

COOK
8 TO 9 HOURS

$\frac{1}{4}$ cup all-purpose flour

1 teaspoon dried thyme leaves, crushed

$1\frac{3}{4}$ pounds skinless, boneless chicken thighs, cut into 1-inch pieces

2 tablespoons vegetable oil

1 pound smoked sausage, cut into 1-inch pieces

1 can ($10\frac{3}{4}$ ounces) Campbell's® Condensed Cream of Celery Soup (Regular **or** 98% Fat Free)

1 can ($10\frac{1}{2}$ ounces) Campbell's® Condensed Chicken Broth

1 can (about $14\frac{1}{2}$ ounces) diced tomatoes

2 teaspoons hot pepper sauce

1 large onion, chopped (about 1 cup)

1 large green pepper, chopped (about 1 cup)

3 stalks celery, sliced (about $1\frac{1}{2}$ cups)

2 bay leaves

1 package (10 ounces) frozen cut okra, thawed

Hot cooked rice (optional)

Campbell's Kitchen Tip

You can also stir $\frac{1}{2}$ **pound** of cooked medium shrimp into the cooker during the last 30 minutes of the cook time.

1. Mix the flour and thyme in a resealable plastic bag. Add the chicken and shake to coat.

2. Heat the oil in a 12-inch skillet over medium-high heat. Add the chicken and cook until it's well browned. Remove the chicken from the skillet. Add the sausage to the skillet and cook until it's well browned.

3. Stir the chicken, sausage, soup, broth, tomatoes, hot pepper sauce, onion, green pepper, celery, bay leaves and okra in a $5\frac{1}{2}$- to 6-quart slow cooker.

4. Cover and cook on LOW for 8 to 9 hours* or until the chicken is cooked through. Remove the bay leaves. Serve with the rice, if desired.

*Or on HIGH for 4 to 5 hours.

Savory Barley & Tomato Soup

MAKES 6 SERVINGS

PREP
15 MINUTES

COOK
6 TO 7 HOURS

1 can (10¾ ounces) Campbell's® Condensed Golden Mushroom Soup

1 can (10½ ounces) Campbell's® Condensed Chicken Broth

1 can (about 28 ounces) diced tomatoes

2 soup cans water

2 large onions, diced (about 2 cups)

2 cloves garlic, minced

3 large carrots, diced (about 1½ cups)

½ cup **uncooked** pearl barley

1 teaspoon dried Italian seasoning, crushed

2 tablespoons chopped fresh parsley

1 cup grated Parmesan cheese

Croutons (optional)

Campbell's Kitchen Tip

*Stir in some Swanson® Chicken Broth **or** water to adjust the consistency, if desired.*

1. Stir soup, broth, tomatoes, water, onions, garlic, carrots, barley and Italian seasoning in a 6-quart slow cooker.

2. Cover and cook on LOW for 6 to 7 hours* or until the barley is tender, stirring once during cooking. Stir in the parsley and cheese. Top with the croutons and additional Parmesan cheese, if desired.

Or on HIGH for 4 to 5 hours.

Panama Pork Stew

MAKES 8 SERVINGS

PREP
20 MINUTES

COOK
7 TO 8 HOURS

2 cups Swanson® Chicken Broth (Regular, Natural Goodness™ **or** Certified Organic)

4 medium sweet potatoes, peeled and cut into 2-inch pieces

2 medium green peppers, cut into 1-inch pieces (about 2 cups)

1½ cups frozen whole kernel corn, thawed

1 large onion, chopped (about 1 cup)

4 cloves garlic, minced

1 can (about 14½ ounces) diced tomatoes with green chiles

¼ cup chopped fresh cilantro leaves

1 teaspoon chili powder

2 pounds boneless pork shoulder, cut into 1-inch pieces

1. Stir the broth, sweet potatoes, peppers, corn, onion, garlic, tomatoes, cilantro, chili powder and pork in a 4½- to 5-quart slow cooker.

2. Cover and cook on LOW for 7 to 8 hours* or until the pork is fork-tender.

Or on HIGH for 4 to 5 hours.

Bacon Potato Chowder

MAKES 8 SERVINGS

PREP
15 MINUTES

COOK
3 TO 4 HOURS

4 slices bacon, cooked and crumbled

1 large onion, chopped (about 1 cup)

4 cans (10¾ ounces **each**) Campbell's® Condensed Cream of Potato Soup

4 soup cans milk

¼ teaspoon ground black pepper

2 large russet potatoes, cut into ½-inch pieces (about 3 cups)

½ cup chopped fresh chives

2 cups shredded Cheddar cheese (about 8 ounces)

1. Stir the bacon, onion, soup, milk, black pepper, potatoes and ¼ **cup** chives in a 6-quart slow cooker.

2. Cover and cook on HIGH for 3 to 4 hours or until the potatoes are tender.

3. Add the cheese and stir until the cheese is melted. Serve with the remaining chives.

Creamy Chicken Tortilla Soup

MAKES 6 SERVINGS

PREP
15 MINUTES

COOK
4 TO 5 HOURS,
15 MINUTES

1 cup Pace® Thick & Chunky Salsa

2 cans (10¾ ounces **each**) Campbell's® Condensed Cream of Chicken Soup (Regular **or** 98% Fat Free)

1 pound skinless, boneless chicken breasts, cut into ½-inch pieces

2 cups frozen whole kernel corn

1 can (about 15 ounces) black beans, rinsed and drained

1 soup can water

1 teaspoon ground cumin

4 corn tortillas (6-inch), cut into strips

1 cup shredded Cheddar cheese (about 4 ounces)

⅓ cup chopped fresh cilantro leaves

1. Stir the salsa, soup, chicken, corn, beans, water and cumin in a 4-quart slow cooker.

2. Cover and cook on LOW for 4 to 5 hours* or until the chicken is cooked through.

3. Stir the tortillas, **1 cup** of the cheese and cilantro into the cooker. Cover and cook for 15 minutes. Serve with additional cheese, if desired.

Or on HIGH for 2 to 2½ hours.

Chipotle Chili

MAKES 8 SERVINGS

PREP
15 MINUTES

COOK
8 TO 9 HOURS

1 jar (16 ounces) Pace® Chipotle Chunky Salsa

1 cup water

2 tablespoons chili powder

1 large onion, chopped (about 1 cup)

2 pounds beef for stew, cut into ½-inch pieces

1 can (about 19 ounces) red kidney beans, rinsed and drained

Shredded Cheddar cheese (optional)

Sour cream (optional)

1. Stir the salsa, water, chili powder, onion, beef and beans in a 3½-quart slow cooker.

2. Cover and cook on LOW for 8 to 9 hours* or until the beef is fork-tender. Serve with the cheese and sour cream, if desired.

Or on HIGH for 4 to 5 hours.

Fennel Soup au Gratin

MAKES 8 SERVINGS

PREP
15 MINUTES

COOK
5 TO 6 HOURS

8 cups Swanson® Beef Broth (Regular, 50% Less Sodium **or** Certified Organic)

2 tablespoons dry sherry

2 teaspoons dried thyme leaves, crushed

3 tablespoons butter

1 bulb fennel, sliced (about 4 cups)

2 large onions, sliced (about 4 cups)

8 slices French bread, about ½ inch thick

½ cup shredded Italian blend cheese

1. Stir the broth, sherry, thyme, butter, fennel and onions in a 5½-quart slow cooker. Cover and cook on HIGH for 5 to 6 hours or until the vegetables are tender.

2. Place the bread slices on a baking sheet. Top **each** bread slice with **1 tablespoon** of the cheese. Broil 4 inches from the heat for 1 minute or until the cheese is melted.

3. Divide the soup mixture among **8** serving bowls. Top **each** with **1** cheese toast.

Yellow Split Pea Soup with Andouille Sausage

MAKES 6 SERVINGS

PREP
15 MINUTES

COOK
4 TO 5 HOURS,
10 MINUTES

5 cups Swanson® Chicken Broth (Regular, Natural Goodness™ **or** Certified Organic)

3 medium carrots, thinly sliced (about 1½ cups)

3 stalks celery, thinly sliced (about 1½ cups)

1 large red onion, finely chopped (about 1 cup)

¼ cup chopped fresh parsley

4 cloves garlic, chopped

1 bay leaf

2 cups dried yellow split peas

6 ounces andouille sausage, diced (about 1½ cups)

1. Stir the broth, carrots, celery, onion, parsley, garlic, bay leaf, peas and sausage in a 3½- to 6-quart slow cooker.

2. Cover and cook on HIGH for 4 to 5 hours* or until the vegetables are tender. Remove the bay leaf.

3. Place ⅓ of the broth mixture into an electric blender or food processor container. Cover and blend until almost smooth. Pour the mixture into a 3-quart saucepan. Repeat the blending process twice more with the remaining broth mixture. Cook over medium heat until the mixture is hot.

Or on LOW for 7 to 8 hours.

Winter Squash Soup

MAKES 8 SERVINGS

PREP
20 MINUTES

COOK
7 TO 8 HOURS,
10 MINUTES

5¼ cups Swanson® Chicken Broth (Regular, Natural
    Goodness™ **or** Certified Organic)

¼ cup packed brown sugar

2 tablespoons minced fresh ginger root

1 cinnamon stick

1 butternut squash (about 1¾ pounds), peeled,
    seeded and cut into 1-inch pieces (about 4 cups)

1 large acorn squash, peeled, seeded and cut into
    1-inch pieces (about 3½ cups)

1 large sweet onion, coarsely chopped (about
    1 cup)

1. Stir the broth, brown sugar, ginger, cinnamon stick, squash and onion in a 6-quart slow cooker.

2. Cover and cook on LOW for 7 to 8 hours* or until the squash is tender.

3. Remove the cinnamon stick. Place ⅓ of the squash mixture into an electric blender or food processor container. Cover and blend until smooth. Pour the mixture into a 3-quart saucepan. Repeat the blending process twice more with the remaining squash mixture. Cook over medium heat until the mixture is hot.

Creamy Winter Squash Soup: Stir in ½ **cup** of half-and-half before reheating the soup in step 3.

Spicy Verde Chicken & Bean Chili

MAKES 6 SERVINGS

PREP
10 MINUTES

COOK
2 HOURS, 15 MINUTES

2 tablespoons butter

1 large onion, chopped (about 1 cup)

¼ teaspoon garlic powder **or** 2 cloves garlic , minced

2 cups Swanson® Chicken Broth (Regular, Natural Goodness™ **or** Certified Organic)

2 cups shredded cooked chicken

1 can (about 16 ounces) small white beans, undrained

1 can (4 ounces) Pace® Diced Green Chiles, drained

1 teaspoon ground cumin

1 teaspoon jalapeño hot pepper sauce

1 tablespoon all-purpose flour

1 tablespoon water

6 flour tortillas (8-inch), warmed

Shredded Monterey Jack cheese (optional)

Chopped fresh cilantro leaves (optional)

1. Heat the butter in a 12-inch skillet over medium heat. Add the onion and garlic powder and cook until the onion is tender, stirring occasionally.

2. Stir the onion, broth, chicken, beans, chiles, cumin and hot pepper sauce in a 5-quart slow cooker. Cover and cook on HIGH for 2 hours.

3. Stir the flour and water in a small cup. Stir into the cooker. Cover and cook for 15 minutes or until the mixture boils and thickens.

4. Place the tortillas into **6** serving bowls. Divide the chili among the bowls. Top with the cheese and cilantro, if desired.

Southwestern Chicken & White Bean Soup

MAKES 6 SERVINGS

PREP
15 MINUTES

COOK
8 TO 9 HOURS

1 tablespoon vegetable oil

1 pound skinless, boneless chicken breasts, cut into 1-inch pieces

1¾ cups Swanson® Chicken Broth (Regular, Natural Goodness™ **or** Certified Organic)

1 cup Pace® Thick & Chunky Salsa

3 cloves garlic, minced

2 teaspoons ground cumin

1 can (about 16 ounces) small white beans, rinsed and drained

1 cup frozen whole kernel corn

1 large onion, chopped (about 1 cup)

1. Heat the oil in a 10-inch skillet over medium-high heat. Add the chicken and cook until it's well browned, stirring often.

2. Stir the chicken, broth, salsa, garlic, cumin, beans, corn and onion in a 3½-quart slow cooker.

3. Cover and cook on LOW for 8 to 9 hours* or until the chicken is cooked through.

Or on HIGH for 4 to 5 hours.

Slow-Simmered Chicken Rice Soup

MAKES 8 SERVINGS

PREP
15 MINUTES

COOK
7 TO 8 HOURS,
15 MINUTES

½ cup **uncooked** wild rice

½ cup **uncooked** regular long-grain white rice

1 tablespoon vegetable oil

5¼ cups Swanson® Chicken Broth (Regular, Natural Goodness™ **or** Certified Organic)

2 teaspoons dried thyme leaves, crushed

¼ teaspoon crushed red pepper

2 stalks celery, coarsely chopped (about 1 cup)

1 medium onion, chopped (about ½ cup)

1 pound skinless, boneless chicken breasts, cut into cubes

Sour cream (optional)

Chopped green onions (optional)

Time-Saving Tip

*Speed preparation by substituting 3 cans (4.5 ounces **each**) Swanson® Premium Chunk Chicken Breast, drained, for the raw chicken.*

1. Stir the wild rice, white rice and oil in a 3½-quart slow cooker. Cover and cook on HIGH for 15 minutes.

2. Add the broth, thyme, red pepper, celery, onion and chicken to the cooker. Turn the heat to LOW. Cover and cook for 7 to 8 hours* or until the chicken is cooked through.

3. Serve with the sour cream and green onions, if desired.

Or on HIGH for 4 to 5 hours.

Poblano Corn Chowder with Chicken and Chorizo

MAKES 8 SERVINGS

PREP
15 MINUTES

COOK
7 TO 8 HOURS

Campbell's Kitchen Tip

To enhance the flavor of the chowder, roast the chiles and corn before adding to the cooker. Place the chiles and thawed corn in a single layer in a roasting pan. Drizzle with 1 tablespoon olive oil. Toss to coat. Bake at 375°F. for 30 minutes.

4 cups Swanson® Chicken Broth (Regular, Natural Goodness™ **or** Certified Organic)

1 tablespoon sugar

2 cans (14½ ounces **each**) cream-style corn

1 large potato, diced (about 2 cups)

2 large poblano chiles, seeded and diced (about 2 cups)

1 package (10 ounces) frozen whole kernel corn, thawed

1 pound skinless, boneless chicken breasts **and/or** thighs, cut into cubes

½ pound chorizo sausage, diced

1 cup heavy cream

¼ cup chopped fresh cilantro leaves

1. Stir the broth, sugar, canned corn, potato, chiles, frozen corn, chicken and sausage in a 6-quart slow cooker.

2. Cover and cook on LOW for 7 to 8 hours* or until the chicken is cooked through. Stir in the cream and cilantro.

Or on HIGH for 4 to 5 hours.

Chili Pork Stew

MAKES 6 SERVINGS

PREP
25 MINUTES

COOK
7 TO 8 HOURS

1½ pounds boneless pork shoulder, cut into 1-inch pieces

2 tablespoons all-purpose flour

2 tablespoons vegetable oil

2 cups Swanson® Chicken Broth (Regular, Natural Goodness™ **or** Certified Organic)

2 tablespoons chili powder

1 teaspoon ground cumin

1 teaspoon hot pepper sauce

2 cloves garlic, minced

1 can (about 28 ounces) diced tomatoes

2 large potatoes, cut into 2-inch pieces

1 large green pepper, chopped (about 1 cup)

1 large onion, chopped (about 1 cup)

1 can (about 15 ounces) red kidney beans, rinsed and drained

1. Place the pork in a large bowl. Add the flour and toss to coat.

2. Heat the oil in a 12-inch skillet over medium-high heat. Add the pork and cook until it's well browned. Remove the pork from the skillet.

3. Stir the broth, chili powder, cumin, hot pepper sauce and garlic into the skillet. Heat to a boil, stirring often.

4. Stir the broth mixture, pork, tomatoes, potatoes, pepper, onion and beans in a 4- to 6-quart slow cooker.

5. Cover and cook on LOW for 7 to 8 hours* or until the pork is fork-tender.

Or on HIGH for 4 to 5 hours.

Veal Stew with Garden Vegetables

MAKES 6 SERVINGS

2 to 2½ pounds veal for stew, cut into 1-inch pieces*

Ground black pepper

2 tablespoons olive oil

1 bag (16 ounces) fresh **or** frozen whole baby carrots

1 large onion, diced (about 1 cup)

4 cloves garlic, minced

¼ cup all-purpose flour

2 cups Swanson® Chicken Broth (Regular, Natural Goodness™ **or** Certified Organic)

½ teaspoon dried rosemary leaves, crushed

1 can (about 14½ ounces) diced tomatoes

1 cup frozen peas, thawed

Hot cooked rice **or** barley

PREP
15 MINUTES

COOK
7 TO 8 HOURS

1. Season the veal with the black pepper.

2. Heat the oil in a 12-inch skillet over medium-high heat. Add the veal and cook in 2 batches until it's well browned, stirring often.

3. Place the veal, carrots, onion and garlic into a 3½- to 6-quart slow cooker. Sprinkle with the flour and toss to coat.

4. Add the broth, rosemary and tomatoes. Cover and cook on LOW for 7 to 8 hours**.

5. Add the peas to the cooker. Cover and cook for 1 hour or until the veal is fork-tender. Serve with the rice.

*You can substitute skinless, boneless chicken thighs, cut into 1-inch pieces, for the veal.

**Or on HIGH for 4 to 5 hours.

Campbell's Kitchen Tip

For more flavorful rice or barley, cook it in Swanson® Chicken Broth.

Slow Cooker Party Foods

Chicken & Vegetable Bruschetta

MAKES 7 CUPS

PREP
15 MINUTES

COOK
6 TO 7 HOURS

STAND
5 MINUTES

1 can (10¾ ounces) Campbell's® Condensed Cream of Mushroom Soup (Regular, 98% Fat Free **or** 25% Less Sodium)

1 can (about 14½ ounces) diced tomatoes, drained

1 small eggplant, peeled and diced (about 2 cups)

1 large zucchini, diced (about 2 cups)

1 small onion, chopped (about ¼ cup)

1 pound skinless, boneless chicken breasts

¼ cup shredded Parmesan cheese

2 tablespoons chopped fresh parsley **or** basil leaves

Thinly sliced Italian bread, toasted

Campbell's Kitchen Tip

The chicken mixture is also delicious over hot cooked rice or pasta

1. Stir the soup, tomatoes, eggplant, zucchini and onion in a 6-quart slow cooker. Add the chicken and turn to coat.

2. Cover and cook on LOW for 6 to 7 hours* or until the chicken is fork-tender.

3. Remove the chicken from the cooker to a cutting board and let stand for 5 minutes. Using 2 forks, shred the chicken. Return the chicken to the cooker. Stir in the cheese and parsley.

4. Serve on the bread slices. Sprinkle with additional Parmesan cheese and chopped parsley, if desired.

Or on HIGH for 4 to 5 hours.

Swiss Cheese Fondue

MAKES 6 SERVINGS

PREP
10 MINUTES

COOK
1 HOUR

1 clove garlic, cut in half

1 can (10½ ounces) Campbell's® Condensed Chicken Broth

2 cans (10¾ ounces **each**) Campbell's® Condensed Cheddar Cheese Soup

1 cup water

½ cup Chablis **or** other dry white wine

1 tablespoon Dijon-style mustard

1 tablespoon cornstarch

1 pound shredded Emmentaler **or** Gruyère cheese, at room temperature

¼ teaspoon ground nutmeg

Dash ground black pepper

Pepperidge Farm® Hearth Fired Artisan Bread, any variety **or** Pepperidge Farm® Garlic Bread, baked and cut into cubes

Fresh vegetables for dipping

Campbell's Kitchen Tip

This recipe may be doubled.

1. Rub the inside of a 5½- to 6-quart slow cooker with the cut sides of the garlic. Discard the garlic. Stir the broth, soup, water, wine, mustard, cornstarch, cheese, nutmeg and black pepper in the cooker.

2. Cover and cook on LOW for 1 hour or until the cheese is melted, stirring occasionally.

3. Serve with the bread and vegetables on skewers for dipping.

Slow-Cooked Mini Pulled Pork Bites

MAKES 16 MINI SANDWICHES

PREP
10 MINUTES

COOK
6 TO 7 HOURS

STAND
10 MINUTES

1 can (10¾ ounces) Campbell's® Condensed Tomato Soup

½ cup packed brown sugar

¼ cup cider vinegar

1 teaspoon garlic powder

4 pounds boneless pork shoulder

1 package (13.9 ounces) Pepperidge Farm® Soft Country Style Dinner Rolls

Hot pepper sauce (optional)

1. Stir the soup, brown sugar, vinegar and garlic powder in a 6-quart slow cooker. Add the pork and turn to coat.

2. Cover and cook on LOW for 6 to 7 hours* or until the pork is fork-tender.

3. Remove the pork from the cooker to a cutting board and let stand for 10 minutes. Using 2 forks, shred the pork. Return the pork to the cooker.

4. Divide the pork mixture among the rolls. Serve with the hot pepper sauce, if desired.

Or on HIGH for 4 to 5 hours.

Easy Party Meatballs

MAKES 8 SERVINGS

PREP
5 MINUTES

COOK
6 TO 7 HOURS

1 jar (1 pound 10 ounces) Prego® Marinara Italian Sauce

1 jar (12 ounces) grape jelly

½ cup prepared chili sauce

2½ pounds frozen fully-cooked meatballs, cocktail size

Campbell's Kitchen Tips

Larger-size or turkey meatballs can also be used, if desired.

For a special touch, serve with cranberry chutney for dipping.

1. Stir the Italian sauce, jelly, chili sauce and meatballs in a 4½-quart slow cooker.

2. Cover and cook on LOW for 6 to 7 hours* or until the meatballs are cooked through. Serve the meatballs on a serving plate with toothpicks.

Or on HIGH for 3 to 4 hours.

Mahogany Wings

MAKES 18 SERVINGS

PREP
30 MINUTES

MARINATE
6 HOURS

COOK
4 TO 5 HOURS

1 can (10½ ounces) Campbell's® Condensed Beef Broth

2 bunches green onions, chopped

1 cup soy sauce

1 cup plum sauce

6 cloves garlic, minced

½ cup light molasses **or** honey

¼ cup cider vinegar

6 pounds chicken wings

1 tablespoon cornstarch

1. Stir the broth, onions, soy sauce, plum sauce, garlic, molasses and vinegar in a 6-quart slow cooker removable insert.*

2. Cut off the chicken wing tips and discard. Cut the chicken wings in half at the joint. Add the chicken to the cooker and stir to coat. Cover and refrigerate for 6 hours or overnight.

3. Stir ½ **cup** of the marinade and cornstarch in a small bowl. Stir into the chicken mixture.

4. Cover and cook on HIGH for 4 to 5 hours** or until the chicken is cooked through.

*If your slow cooker doesn't have a removable insert, you can stir the marinade ingredients into a large bowl instead. Add the chicken and stir to coat. Cover and refrigerate as directed. Pour the chicken mixture into the cooker and proceed with Steps 3 and 4 as directed.

**Or on LOW for 7 to 8 hours.

Scalloped Potatoes

MAKES 6 SERVINGS

PREP
15 MINUTES

COOK
4 TO 5 HOURS

STAND
5 MINUTES

Vegetable cooking spray

3 pounds Yukon Gold **or** Eastern potatoes, thinly sliced (about 9 cups)

1 large onion, thinly sliced (about 1 cup)

1 can (10¾ ounces) Campbell's® Condensed Cream of Mushroom Soup (Regular, 98% Fat Free **or** 25% Less Sodium)

½ cup Campbell's® Condensed Chicken Broth

1 cup shredded Cheddar **or** crumbled blue cheese (about 4 ounces)

1. Spray the inside of a 6-quart slow cooker with the cooking spray. Layer a third of the potatoes and half of the onion in the cooker. Repeat the layers. Top with the remaining potatoes.

2. Stir the soup and broth in a small bowl. Pour over the potatoes. Cover and cook on HIGH for 4 to 5 hours or until the potatoes are tender.

3. Top the potatoes with the cheese. Cover and let stand for 5 minutes or until the cheese is melted.

Savory Sausage with Onions and Peppers

MAKES 8 SERVINGS

PREP
15 MINUTES

COOK
7 TO 8 HOURS

2 jars (1 pound 10 ounces **each**) Prego® Traditional Italian Sauce

3 large onions, sliced (about 3 cups)

3 large green **and/or** red peppers, cut into 2-inch-long strips (about 6 cups)

3 pounds sweet **or** hot Italian pork sausage, cut into 4-inch-long pieces

8 long hard rolls, split **or** hot cooked spaghetti
  Grated Parmesan cheese (optional)

Campbell's Kitchen Tip

For more overall flavor and color, brown the sausage before adding to the slow cooker.

1. Stir the Italian sauce, onions, peppers and sausage in a 6-quart slow cooker.

2. Cover and cook on LOW for 7 to 8 hours* or until the sausage is cooked through. Spoon the sausage mixture into the rolls or serve it over the spaghetti. Top with the cheese.

*Or on HIGH for 4 to 5 hours.

Slow-Cooked Taco Shredded Beef

MAKES 16 TACOS

PREP
10 MINUTES

COOK
6 TO 7 HOURS

STAND
10 MINUTES

Campbell's Kitchen Tip

This recipe can be doubled.

1 can (10¾ ounces) Campbell's® Condensed French Onion Soup
1 tablespoon chili powder
½ teaspoon ground cumin
2-pound boneless beef chuck roast
2 tablespoons finely chopped fresh cilantro leaves
1 cup shredded Cheddar cheese (about 4 ounces)
16 taco shells
Shredded lettuce
Sour cream

1. Stir the soup, chili powder and cumin in a 4-quart slow cooker. Add the beef and turn to coat.

2. Cover and cook on LOW for 6 to 7 hours* or until the beef is fork-tender.

3. Remove the beef from the cooker to a cutting board and let it stand for 10 minutes. Using 2 forks, shred the beef. Return the beef to the cooker. Stir the cilantro into the cooker.

4. Spoon about ¼ **cup** of the beef mixture into **each** taco shell. Top **each** with about **1 tablespoon** of the cheese. Top with the lettuce and the sour cream.

Or on HIGH for 4 to 5 hours.

Turkey Fajita Wraps

MAKES 8 SERVINGS

PREP
10 MINUTES

COOK
6 TO 7 HOURS

Campbell's Kitchen Tip

Delicious served with an assortment of additional toppers: sliced green onions, sliced ripe olives, shredded lettuce, sliced jalapeño peppers, sour cream and/or chopped fresh cilantro.

2 cups Pace® Thick & Chunky Salsa

2 large green **and/or** red peppers, cut into 2-inch-long strips (about 4 cups)

1½ cups frozen whole kernel corn, thawed

1 tablespoon chili powder

2 tablespoons lime juice

3 cloves garlic, minced

2 pounds turkey breast cutlets, cut into 4-inch-long strips

16 flour tortillas (8-inch), warmed

Shredded Mexican cheese blend

1. Stir the salsa, peppers, corn, chili powder, lime juice, garlic and turkey in a 4-quart slow cooker.

2. Cover and cook on LOW for 6 to 7 hours* or until the turkey is cooked through.

3. Spoon **about** ½ **cup** of the turkey mixture down the center of **each** tortilla. Top with the cheese. Fold the tortillas around the filling.

Or on HIGH for 3 to 4 hours.

Western Egg Strata

MAKES 12 SERVINGS

PREP
15 MINUTES

COOK
7 TO 8 HOURS

Vegetable cooking spray

8 slices Pepperidge Farm® White Sandwich Bread, cut into cubes

3 cups frozen diced potatoes (hash browns)

1 pound maple-flavored ham steak, diced

1 large onion, chopped (about 1 cup)

1 large green pepper, chopped (about 1 cup)

2 cups shredded Cheddar cheese (about 16 ounces)

1 can (10¾ ounces) Campbell's® Condensed Cream of Mushroom Soup (Regular, 98% Fat Free **or** 25% Less Sodium)

8 eggs

2 cups milk

1. Spray the inside of a 4½- to 5-quart slow cooker with the cooking spray. Layer **half** of the bread cubes, potatoes, ham, onion, pepper and cheese in the cooker. Repeat the layers.

2. Beat the soup, eggs and milk with a fork in a medium bowl. Pour over the bread mixture. Press the bread mixture into the soup mixture to coat.

3. Cover and cook on LOW for 7 to 8 hours or until set.

Cornbread Stuffing with Dried Fruit & Herbs

MAKES 24 SERVINGS

PREP
15 MINUTES

COOK
3 HOURS

Vegetable cooking spray

1 bag (16 ounces) Pepperidge Farm® Cornbread Stuffing

2 cups mixed dried fruit (apples, apricots, cranberries and pears)

2 stalks celery, diced (about 1 cup)

1 large red onion, diced (about 1 cup)

½ teaspoon poultry seasoning

¼ cup chopped fresh parsley

4 cups Swanson® Chicken Broth (Regular, Natural Goodness™ **or** Certified Organic)

1. Spray the inside of a 6-quart slow cooker with the cooking spray. Stir the stuffing, fruit, celery, onion, poultry seasoning, parsley and broth **lightly** in the cooker.

2. Cover and cook on HIGH for 1 hour. Reduce the heat to LOW. Cover and cook for 2 hours. Fluff the stuffing mixture with a fork before serving.

Melt-In-Your-Mouth Short Ribs

MAKES 6 SERVINGS

3 pounds beef short ribs, cut into serving-sized pieces

2 tablespoons packed brown sugar

3 cloves garlic, minced

1 teaspoon dried thyme leaves, crushed

¼ cup all-purpose flour

1 can (10½ ounces) Campbell's® Condensed French Onion Soup

1 bottle (12 fluid ounces) dark ale **or** beer

Hot mashed potatoes **or** egg noodles

PREP
10 MINUTES

COOK
8 TO 9 HOURS

1. Place the beef into a 3½- to 6-quart slow cooker. Add the brown sugar, garlic, thyme and flour. Toss to coat.

2. Stir the soup and ale in a small bowl. Pour over the beef.

3. Cover and cook on LOW for 8 to 9 hours* or until the beef is fork-tender. Serve with the mashed potatoes or noodles.

Or on HIGH for 4 to 5 hours.

Savory Simmered Sloppy Joes

MAKES 18 SANDWICHES

PREP
20 MINUTES

COOK
6 TO 7 HOURS

- 3 pounds ground beef
- 2 cans (10¾ ounces **each**) Campbell's® Condensed Tomato Soup
- 2 medium green peppers, chopped (about 2½ cups)
- 3 medium onions, chopped (about 1½ cups)
- ¼ cup Dijon-style mustard
- 3 tablespoons Worcestershire sauce
- 3 tablespoons cider vinegar
- 2 tablespoons packed brown sugar
- 1 teaspoon ground black pepper
- 18 Pepperidge Farm® Classic Hamburger Buns, split

1. Cook the beef in a 12-inch skillet over medium-high heat until it's well browned, stirring often. Pour off any fat.

2. Stir the beef, soup, green peppers, onions, mustard, Worcestershire sauce, vinegar, brown sugar and black pepper in a 6-quart slow cooker.

3. Cover and cook on LOW for 6 to 7 hours* or until the vegetables are tender. Divide the beef mixture among the buns.

Or on HIGH for 3 to 4 hours.

Slow-Cooked Pulled Pork Sandwiches

MAKES 12 SANDWICHES

1 tablespoon vegetable oil

3½- to 4-pound boneless pork shoulder roast, netted **or** tied

1 can (10½ ounces) Campbell's® Condensed French Onion Soup

1 cup ketchup

¼ cup cider vinegar

3 tablespoons packed brown sugar

12 round sandwich rolls **or** hamburger rolls, split

PREP
15 MINUTES

COOK
8 TO 9 HOURS

STAND
10 MINUTES

1. Heat the oil in a 10-inch skillet over medium-high heat. Add the pork and cook until it's well browned on all sides.

2. Stir the soup, ketchup, vinegar and brown sugar in a 5-quart slow cooker. Add the pork and turn to coat.

3. Cover and cook on LOW for 8 to 9 hours* or until the pork is fork-tender.

4. Remove the pork from the cooker to a cutting board and let stand for 10 minutes. Using 2 forks, shred the pork. Return the pork to the cooker.

5. Divide the pork and sauce mixture among the rolls.

*Or on HIGH for 4 to 5 hours.

Jim's Drunken Dogs

MAKES 27 SERVINGS

PREP
5 MINUTES

COOK
2 TO 3 HOURS

3 pounds smoked cocktail frankfurters

2 cans (10¾ ounces **each**) Campbell's® Condensed Tomato Soup

¼ cup packed dark brown sugar

1 cup bourbon

2 tablespoons cider vinegar

1 teaspoon garlic powder

1 tablespoon Worcestershire sauce

1. Stir the frankfurters, soup, brown sugar, bourbon, vinegar, garlic powder and Worcestershire in a 4- to 6-quart slow cooker.

2. Cover and cook on HIGH for 2 to 3 hours or until the mixture is hot.

Sweet & Spicy Baby Back Ribs

MAKES 8 SERVINGS

PREP
10 MINUTES

COOK
7 TO 8 HOURS

1 jar (11 ounces) Pace® Thick & Chunky Salsa

½ cup peach preserves

⅓ cup soy sauce

1 tablespoon minced fresh ginger root

4 pounds pork baby back ribs, cut into serving-sized pieces

1. Stir the salsa, preserves, soy sauce and ginger in a 6-quart slow cooker. Add the ribs and turn to coat.

2. Cover and cook on LOW for 7 to 8 hours* or until the ribs are fork-tender.

*Or on HIGH for 4 to 5 hours.

Sweet 'n' Spicy Barbecued Brisket

MAKES 10 SERVINGS

5-pound trimmed beef brisket
Ground black pepper
1 tablespoon garlic powder
2 cups Pace® Thick & Chunky Salsa **or** Chipotle Chunky Salsa
½ cup packed brown sugar
½ cup Worcestershire sauce
10 sandwich rolls **or** hamburger rolls, split
Prepared coleslaw

PREP
10 MINUTES

MARINATE
8 HOURS

COOK
8 TO 9 HOURS

STAND
10 MINUTES

1. Season the beef with the black pepper and garlic powder and place into a 13×9×2-inch shallow baking dish.

2. Stir the salsa, brown sugar and Worcestershire in a small bowl. Spread the salsa mixture over the beef. Cover and refrigerate at least 8 hours or overnight.

3. Place the beef into a 7-quart slow cooker. Cover and cook on LOW for 8 to 9 hours* or until the beef is fork-tender. Remove the beef from the cooker to a cutting board and let stand for 10 minutes.

4. Thinly slice the beef across the grain, or using 2 forks, shred the beef. Return the beef to the cooker. Divide the beef and juices among the rolls. Top the beef with the coleslaw.

Or on HIGH for 4 to 5 hours.

Slow-Cooked Parmesan Chicken

MAKES 6 SERVINGS

PREP
5 MINUTES

COOK
8 TO 9 HOURS

Vegetable cooking spray

6 skinless, boneless chicken breast halves (about 1½ pounds)

6 tablespoons butter **or** margarine

1 package (1 ounce) Campbell's® Dry Onion Soup & Recipe Mix

2 cans (10¾ ounces **each**) Campbell's® Condensed Cream of Mushroom Soup (Regular, 98% Fat Free **or** 25% Less Sodium)

1½ cups milk

1 cup converted long-grain white rice

¼ cup grated Parmesan cheese

1. Spray the inside of a 4-quart slow cooker with the cooking spray. Place the chicken into the cooker. Place **1 tablespoon** of butter onto **each** chicken breast half.

2. Stir the onion soup mix, mushroom soup, milk and rice in a medium bowl. Pour over the chicken. Sprinkle with the cheese.

3. Cover and cook on LOW for 8 to 9 hours* or until the chicken is cooked through.

Or on HIGH for 4 to 5 hours.

Chipotle Mini Meatballs

MAKES 6 SERVINGS

1 tablespoon vegetable oil

2 pounds frozen fully-cooked meatballs, cocktail size

2 cans (10¾ ounces **each**) Campbell's® Condensed Tomato Soup

1 can (10½ ounces) Campbell's® Condensed Chicken Broth

2 chipotle chiles in adobe sauce, chopped

1 large onion, chopped (about 1 cup)

3 cloves garlic, minced

2 teaspoons chili powder

2 tablespoons soy sauce

¼ cup honey

¼ cup cider vinegar

Chopped fresh cilantro leaves

PREP
15 MINUTES

COOK
4 TO 5 HOURS

1. Heat the oil in a 12-inch skillet over medium-high heat. Add the meatballs and cook in 2 batches until they're well browned. Pour off any fat.

2. Stir the meatballs, soup, broth, chiles, onion, garlic, chili powder, soy sauce, honey and vinegar in a 5½- to 6-quart slow cooker.

3. Cover and cook on LOW for 4 to 5 hours or until the meatballs are cooked through. Sprinkle with the cilantro. Serve the meatballs on a serving plate with toothpicks.

Time-Saving Tip

To save preparation time, you can omit the oil and skip the browning of the meatballs in Step 1. Stir the meatballs into the cooker as directed in Step 2.

Worldly Possibilities

Asian Glazed Short Ribs

MAKES 8 SERVINGS

PREP
10 MINUTES

COOK
6 TO 7 HOURS

1½ cups Swanson® Beef Broth (Regular, 50% Less Sodium **or** Certified Organic)

½ cup orange marmalade

⅓ cup chili sauce

2 tablespoons soy sauce

1 medium onion, thinly sliced (about ½ cup)

4 to 5 pounds beef short ribs

Hot cooked jasmine **or** basmati rice

1. Stir the broth, marmalade, chili sauce, soy sauce and onion in a 6-quart slow cooker. Add the beef and turn to coat.

2. Cover and cook on LOW for 6 to 7 hours or until the beef is fork-tender. Serve with the rice.

Spaghetti Bolognese

MAKES 8 SERVINGS

PREP
15 MINUTES

COOK
4 TO 5 HOURS

6 slices bacon, cut into ½-inch pieces
1 large onion, diced (about 1 cup)
3 cloves garlic, minced
2 pounds ground beef
4 cups Prego® Traditional Italian Sauce
1 cup milk
1 pound spaghetti, cooked and drained*
Grated Parmesan cheese

1. Cook the bacon in a 12-inch skillet over medium-high heat until it's crisp. Remove the bacon from the skillet. Pour off all but **1 tablespoon** of the drippings.

2. Add the onion and cook in the hot drippings until tender. Add the garlic and beef and cook until the beef is well browned, stirring often. Pour off any fat.

3. Stir the bacon, beef mixture, Italian sauce and milk in a 6-quart slow cooker.

4. Cover and cook on HIGH for 4 to 5 hours**. Toss the spaghetti with the sauce.

*Reserve some of the cooking water from the spaghetti. You can use it to adjust the consistency of the finished sauce, if you like.

**Or on LOW for 7 to 8 hours.

Caponata

MAKES 6 CUPS

PREP
20 MINUTES

COOK
7 TO 8 HOURS

4 cups eggplant cut into 1-inch cubes

1 large onion, diced (about 1 cup)

1 can (10¾ ounces) Campbell's® Condensed Golden Mushroom Soup

1 can (about 14½ ounces) diced tomatoes

2 stalks celery, diced (about 1 cup)

½ cup sliced green olives

2 tablespoons balsamic vinegar

1 tablespoon tomato paste

1 clove garlic, minced

½ teaspoon dried oregano leaves, crushed

¼ teaspoon crushed red pepper

Hot cooked penne pasta

Shredded Parmesan cheese

Campbell's Kitchen Tip

The caponata is also delicious served in pita bread, topped with crumbled feta cheese.

1. Stir the eggplant, onion, soup, tomatoes, celery, olives, vinegar, tomato paste, garlic, oregano and red pepper in a 6-quart slow cooker.

2. Cover and cook on LOW for 7 to 8 hours* or until the vegetables are tender. Serve over the pasta. Sprinkle with the cheese.

Or on HIGH for 4 to 5 hours.

West African Chicken Stew

MAKES 6 SERVINGS

PREP
15 MINUTES

COOK
7 TO 8 HOURS

½ cup all-purpose flour

1 teaspoon paprika

2 teaspoons pumpkin pie spice

½ teaspoon cracked black pepper

6 bone-in chicken thighs

6 chicken drumsticks

2 tablespoons vegetable oil

1 can (10¾ ounces) Campbell's® Condensed French Onion Soup

½ cup water

1 cup raisins*

½ cup orange juice

1 teaspoon grated orange peel

2 tablespoons chopped fresh parsley **or** cilantro leaves

6 cups hot cooked couscous

1. Mix the flour, paprika, pumpkin pie spice and black pepper on a plate. Coat the chicken with the flour mixture.

2. Heat the oil in a 12-inch skillet over medium heat. Add the chicken and cook for 10 minutes or until it's well browned.

3. Stir the soup, water, raisins, orange juice and orange peel in a 6-quart slow cooker. Add the chicken and turn to coat.

4. Cover and cook on LOW for 7 to 8 hours** or until the chicken is cooked through.

5. Stir the parsley into the cooker. Serve with the couscous.

*You can substitute chopped prunes **or** apricots for the raisins, if you like.

**Or on HIGH for 4 to 5 hours.

Corned Beef & Cabbage

MAKES 10 SERVINGS

PREP
20 MINUTES

COOK
8 TO 9 HOURS

Campbell's Kitchen Tip

*For thicker sauce: Remove the beef and vegetables from the cooker. Stir **2 tablespoons** cornstarch and **2 tablespoons** water in a small bowl. Add to the cooker and cook on HIGH for 15 minutes or until the mixture boils and thickens.*

3½ cups Swanson® Beef Broth (Regular, 50% Less Sodium **or** Certified Organic)
¼ cup cider vinegar
2 medium onions, cut into quarters
5 medium potatoes, peeled and cut into quarters (about 5 cups)
5 medium carrots, cut into 2-inch pieces (about 2½ cups)
3 pounds corned beef **or** beef brisket
1 head green cabbage, trimmed and cut into 6 wedges (about 2 pounds)
   Bouquet Garni

1. Stir the broth and vinegar in a 6-quart slow cooker. Add the onions, potatoes, carrots, beef and cabbage. Submerge the *Bouquet Garni* in the broth mixture.

2. Cover and cook on LOW for 8 to 9 hours* or until the beef is fork-tender. Remove the *Bouquet Garni*.

Bouquet Garni: Lay a **4-inch square** of cheesecloth flat on the counter. Place **4 cloves** garlic, **1 tablespoon** pickling spice and **2** bay leaves in the center of the cloth. Bring the corners of the cheesecloth together and tie with kitchen string into a bundle.

Or on HIGH for 4 to 5 hours.

Picadillo

MAKES 8 SERVINGS

PREP
15 MINUTES

COOK
7 TO 8 HOURS

1½ pounds ground beef

2 large onions, diced (about 2 cups)

1¾ cups Swanson® Beef Broth (Regular, 50% Less Sodium **or** Certified Organic)

1 jar (11 ounces) Pace® Thick & Chunky Salsa

1 tablespoon tomato paste

1 tablespoon chili powder

1 teaspoon ground cumin

½ cup raisins

½ cup toasted slivered almonds

Hot cooked rice

1. Cook the beef and onions in a 12-inch skillet over medium-high heat until the beef is well browned, stirring often. Pour off any fat.

2. Stir the beef mixture, broth, salsa, tomato paste, chili powder, cumin and raisins in a 6-quart slow cooker.

3. Cover and cook on LOW for 7 to 8 hours*. Top the beef mixture with the almonds. Serve with the rice.

*Or on HIGH for 4 to 5 hours.

Moroccan Brisket with Onions & Apricots

MAKES 8 SERVINGS

PREP
10 MINUTES

COOK
7 TO 8 HOURS

2 large onions, sliced into wedges

2 teaspoons ground coriander (optional)

2 teaspoons ground cumin

½ teaspoon ground cinnamon

½ teaspoon garlic powder

3-pound boneless beef brisket

1 cup dried apricots

1¾ cups Swanson® Beef Broth (Regular, 50% Less Sodium **or** Certified Organic)

2 tablespoons honey

1. Place the onions into a 6-quart slow cooker.

2. Combine the coriander, cumin, cinnamon and garlic powder in a small bowl. Rub the mixture onto the beef. Place the beef into the cooker. Place the apricots around the beef.

3. Stir the broth and honey in a small bowl. Pour over the beef. Cover and cook on LOW for 7 to 8 hours* or until the beef is fork-tender.

*Or on HIGH for 4 to 5 hours.

Chicken & Sausage Paella

MAKES 8 SERVINGS

PREP
15 MINUTES

COOK
6 TO 7 HOURS

1 pound skinless, boneless chicken thighs, cut into cubes

1 pound chorizo sausage **or** Andouille sausage, thinly sliced

2 cups **uncooked** regular long-grain white rice

1 large red onion, chopped (about 1 cup)

3 cups Campbell's® Condensed Chicken Broth

1 can (10¾ ounces) Campbell's® Condensed Tomato Soup

1 cup frozen peas, thawed

½ cup chopped Manzanella olives

2 tablespoons chopped fresh parsley

Campbell's Kitchen Tip

You can top this dish with cooked shrimp before serving, if desired.

1. Stir the chicken, sausage, rice, onion, broth and soup in a 6-quart slow cooker.

2. Cover and cook on LOW for 6 to 7 hours* or until the chicken is cooked through.

3. Stir the peas and olives into the cooker. Cover and cook until the mixture is hot. Sprinkle with the parsley.

Or on HIGH for 4 to 5 hours.

Shredded Pork Burritos with Green Chile Sauce

MAKES 12 BURRITOS

PREP
15 MINUTES

COOK
8 TO 9 HOURS,
25 MINUTES

STAND
10 MINUTES

1 tablespoon vegetable oil
1 large onion, chopped (about 1 cup)
4 cloves garlic, minced
2 jars (16 ounces **each**) Pace® Thick & Chunky Salsa
1 cup water
1 medium red pepper, chopped (about 1 cup)
8 green onions, chopped (about 1 cup)
1 bunch fresh cilantro leaves, chopped (about 1 cup)
¼ cup lemon pepper seasoning
¼ cup ground cumin
¼ cup chili powder
1 tablespoon lime juice
  4-pound boneless pork loin roast, netted **or** tied
1 can (4 ounces) Pace® Diced Green Chiles
12 (10-inch) flour tortillas, warmed
1 package (8 ounces) shredded Monterey Jack cheese (about 2 cups)

1. Heat the oil in a 12-inch skillet over medium heat. Add the onion and garlic and cook until tender. Stir the salsa, water, red pepper, green onions, cilantro, lemon pepper, cumin, chili powder and lime juice into the skillet.

2. Place the pork into a 5-quart slow cooker. Pour the salsa mixture over the pork.

3. Cover and cook on LOW for 8 to 9 hours* or until the pork is fork-tender.

4. Remove the pork from the cooker to a cutting board and let it stand for 10 minutes. Using 2 forks, shred the pork.

5. Spoon **5 cups** of the salsa mixture from the cooker into a 2-quart saucepan. Stir in the chiles. Cook over medium-high heat to a boil. Reduce the heat to medium-low. Cook and stir for 15 minutes or until the mixture thickens.

6. Spoon **1 cup** of the pork down the center of **each** tortilla. Top **each** with **2 tablespoons** of the green chile sauce. Fold the sides of the tortillas over the filling and then fold up the ends to enclose the filling. Divide the remaining green chile sauce and the cheese over the burritos.

Or on HIGH for 4 to 5 hours.

Sauerbraten

MAKES 6 SERVINGS

PREP
15 MINUTES

MARINATE
72 HOURS

COOK
7 TO 8 HOURS

Campbell's Kitchen Tip

For thicker sauce:
Before adding the
raisins and sour cream,
remove the beef from
the slow cooker.
Stir 2 tablespoons
cornstarch and 1 cup
of the sauce from the
cooker in a small bowl.
Stir into the cooker.
Turn the heat to HIGH.
Cover and cook for
15 minutes or until
the mixture boils and
thickens.

2 cups cider vinegar

1 cup packed dark brown sugar

2 large onions, sliced (about 2 cups)

2 large carrots, cut into 2-inch pieces (about 1 cup)

10 gingersnap cookies, crushed

1 can (10½ ounces) Campbell's® Condensed Beef Consommé

   Bouquet Garni

1 cup water

   4- to 5-pound boneless beef rump roast

2 tablespoons vegetable oil

1 cup Burgundy wine

½ cup golden raisins

½ cup sour cream (optional)

1. Heat the vinegar, brown sugar, onions, carrots, gingersnaps, consommé and *Bouquet Garni* in a 2-quart saucepan over medium-high heat to a boil. Remove from the heat. Stir in the water and let cool to room temperature.

2. Place the beef in a large nonmetallic bowl. Add the vinegar mixture and turn to coat. Cover and refrigerate for about 72 hours, turning the beef over in the marinade 1 to 2 times per day.

3. Remove the beef from the bowl and pat dry with paper towels. Reserve the marinade mixture.

4. Heat the oil in a 12-inch skillet over medium-high heat. Add the beef and cook until it's well browned on all sides. Remove the beef from the skillet and place it into a 5- to 6½-quart slow cooker.

5. Add the wine to the skillet and heat to a boil, stirring often. Pour the wine and reserved marinade over the beef.

6. Cover and cook on LOW for 7 to 8 hours* or until the beef is fork-tender. Stir in the raisins and the sour cream, if desired.

Bouquet Garni: Lay a **4-inch square** of cheesecloth flat on the counter. Place ⅓ **cup** of pickling spice in the center of the cloth. Bring the corners of the cloth together and tie with kitchen string into a bundle.

Or on HIGH for 4 to 5 hours.

Asian Tomato Beef

MAKES 8 SERVINGS

PREP
10 MINUTES

COOK
7 TO 8 HOURS,
15 MINUTES

2 cans (10¾ ounces **each**) Campbell's® Condensed Tomato Soup
⅓ cup soy sauce
⅓ cup vinegar
1½ teaspoons garlic powder
¼ teaspoon ground black pepper
3 to 3½ pounds boneless beef round steak, cut into strips
6 cups broccoli flowerets
Hot cooked rice

1. Stir the soup, soy, vinegar, garlic powder, black pepper and beef in a 3½-quart slow cooker.

2. Cover and cook on LOW for 7 to 8 hours* or until the beef is fork-tender.

3. Stir in the broccoli. Turn the heat to HIGH. Cover and cook for 15 minutes or until the broccoli is tender-crisp. Serve with the rice.

*Or on HIGH for 4 to 5 hours.

Chicken Asopao with Smoked Ham and Manchego Cheese

MAKES 8 SERVINGS

4 cups Swanson® Chicken Broth (Regular, Natural Goodness™ **or** Certified Organic)

1 teaspoon dried oregano leaves, crushed

1 large onion, chopped (about 1 cup)

1 large green pepper, chopped (about 1 cup)

1 can (10 ounces) diced tomatoes with green chilies, undrained

1 pound skinless, boneless chicken thighs, cut into cubes

¾ pound cooked ham, diced

2 cups **uncooked** instant white rice

1 tablespoon drained capers

½ cup grated manchego cheese

PREP
15 MINUTES

COOK
6 TO 8 HOURS,
5 MINUTES

1. Stir the broth, oregano, onion, pepper, tomatoes with chilies, chicken and ham in an 8-quart slow cooker.

2. Cover and cook on LOW for 6 to 8 hours*.

3. Stir in the rice and capers. Cover and cook for 5 minutes. Sprinkle with the cheese.

Or on HIGH for 4 to 5 hours.

Easy Substitution Tip

If you are unable to find manchego cheese, use Pecorino Romano or Parmesan cheese.

Worldly Possibilities   119

Persian Split Pea Soup

MAKES 8 SERVINGS

PREP
15 MINUTES

COOK
7 TO 8 HOURS

5 cups Swanson® Chicken Broth (Regular, Natural Goodness™ **or** Certified Organic)
2 pounds beef for stew, cut into 2-inch pieces
3 leeks, cut into 1-inch pieces
1 large onion, chopped (about 1 cup)
1½ cups dried yellow split peas
5 cloves garlic, minced
3 bay leaves
1 teaspoon dried oregano leaves, crushed
2 teaspoons ground cumin
½ cup golden raisins
2 tablespoons lemon juice

Easy Substitution Tip

You can substitute lamb for stew for the beef.

1. Stir the broth, beef, leeks, onion, split peas, garlic, bay leaves, oregano, cumin, raisins and lemon juice in a 6-quart slow cooker.

2. Cover and cook on LOW for 7 to 8 hours or until the beef is fork-tender. Remove the bay leaves.

Greek-Style Beef Stew

MAKES 6 SERVINGS

2 to 2½ pounds boneless beef bottom round roast **or** chuck pot roast, cut into 1-inch pieces

1 bag (16 ounces) frozen whole small white onions

1 bag (16 ounces) fresh **or** frozen whole baby carrots (about 2½ cups)

2 tablespoons all-purpose flour

1¾ cups Swanson® Beef Broth (Regular, 50% Less Sodium **or** Certified Organic)

1 can (5.5 ounces) V8® 100% Vegetable Juice

1 tablespoon packed brown sugar

Bouquet Garni

Hot cooked egg noodles

PREP
10 MINUTES

COOK
8 TO 9 HOURS

1. Place the beef, onions and carrots into a 3½- to 6-quart slow cooker. Sprinkle with the flour and toss to coat.

2. Stir the broth, vegetable juice and brown sugar in a medium bowl. Pour over the beef and vegetables. Submerge the *Bouquet Garni* into the broth mixture.

3. Cover and cook on LOW for 8 to 9 hours* or until the beef is fork-tender. Remove the *Bouquet Garni*. Serve over the noodles.

Bouquet Garni: Lay a **4-inch square** of cheesecloth flat on the counter. Place ½ **teaspoon** whole cloves, **1** cinnamon stick and **1** bay leaf in the center of the cloth. Bring the corners of the cloth together and tie with kitchen string into a bundle.

Or on HIGH for 4 to 5 hours.

Mexican Beef & Bean Stew

MAKES 6 SERVINGS

PREP
15 MINUTES

COOK
8 TO 9 HOURS

1½ pounds beef for stew, cut into 1-inch pieces
2 tablespoons all-purpose flour
1 tablespoon vegetable oil
1 can (10½ ounces) Campbell's® Condensed Beef Consommé
1 cup Pace® Thick & Chunky Salsa
1 large onion, coarsely chopped (about 1 cup)
1 can (about 15 ounces) pinto beans, rinsed and drained
1 can (about 16 ounces) whole kernel corn, drained
2 tablespoons chili powder
1 teaspoon ground cumin
¼ teaspoon garlic powder **or** 2 cloves garlic, minced

1. Coat the beef with flour. Heat the oil in a 12-inch skillet over medium-high heat. Add the beef and cook in 2 batches until it's well browned, stirring often.

2. Stir the beef, consommé, salsa, onion, beans, corn, chili powder, cumin and garlic powder in a 3½-quart slow cooker.

3. Cover and cook on LOW for 8 to 9 hours* or until the beef is fork-tender.

Or on HIGH for 4 to 5 hours.

Jambalaya

MAKES 6 SERVINGS

2 cups Swanson® Chicken Broth (Regular, Natural Goodness™ **or** Certified Organic)

1 tablespoon Creole seasoning

1 large green pepper, diced (about 1⅓ cups)

1 large onion, diced (about 1 cup)

2 large stalks celery, diced (about 1 cup)

1 can (about 14½ ounces) diced tomatoes

1 pound kielbasa, diced

¾ pound skinless, boneless chicken thighs, cut into cubes

1 cup **uncooked** regular long-grain white rice

½ pound fresh medium shrimp, shelled and deveined

PREP
15 MINUTES

COOK
7 TO 8 HOURS,
40 MINUTES

1. Stir the broth, Creole seasoning, pepper, onion, celery, tomatoes, kielbasa, chicken and rice in a 3½- to 6-quart slow cooker.

2. Cover and cook on LOW for 7 to 8 hours*.

3. Add the shrimp. Cover and cook for 40 minutes or until the shrimp are cooked through.

*Or on HIGH for 4 to 5 hours.

Italian Beef Roast

MAKES 6 SERVINGS

PREP
15 MINUTES

COOK
8 TO 9 HOURS,
20 MINUTES

2½-pound boneless beef bottom round roast
  or chuck pot roast

Ground black pepper

1 tablespoon vegetable oil

1 can (10½ ounces) Campbell's® Condensed French
  Onion Soup

1 cup Burgundy wine **or** other dry red wine

¼ cup red wine vinegar

3 cloves garlic, minced

1 teaspoon dried oregano leaves, crushed

1 can (about 14½ ounces) diced tomatoes

1 medium onion, chopped (about ½ cup)

¼ cup sliced pimento-stuffed olives

1. Season the beef with the black pepper. Heat the oil in a 12-inch skillet over medium-high heat. Add the beef and cook until it's well browned on all sides.

2. Stir the soup, wine, vinegar, garlic, oregano, tomatoes and onion in a 3½-quart slow cooker. Add the beef and turn to coat.

3. Cover and cook on LOW for 8 to 9 hours* or until the beef is fork-tender.

4. Remove the beef from the cooker. Stir the olives into the cooker. Turn the heat to HIGH. Cover and cook for 10 minutes. Serve the sauce with the beef.

Or on HIGH for 4 to 5 hours.

Chicken Cacciatore

MAKES 6 SERVINGS

1¾ cups Swanson® Chicken Broth (Regular, Natural Goodness™ **or** Certified Organic)

1 teaspoon garlic powder

2 cans (about 14½ ounces **each**) diced tomatoes with Italian herbs

12 ounces mushrooms, cut in half (about 4 cups)

2 large onions, chopped (about 2 cups)

3 pounds chicken parts, skin removed

Hot cooked spaghetti

1. Mix the broth, garlic powder, tomatoes, mushrooms and onions in a 3½-quart slow cooker. Add the chicken and turn to coat.

2. Cover and cook on LOW for 7 to 8 hours* or until the chicken is cooked through. Serve with the spaghetti.

Or on HIGH for 4 to 5 hours.

PREP
10 MINUTES

COOK
7 TO 8 HOURS

Campbell's Kitchen Tip

For thicker sauce, mix **2 tablespoons** of cornstarch and **2 tablespoons** of water in a small bowl. Remove the chicken from the cooker. Stir the cornstarch mixture into the cooker. Turn the heat to HIGH. Cover and cook for 10 minutes or until the mixture boils and thickens.

Spiced Pot Roast

MAKES 8 SERVINGS

PREP
15 MINUTES

COOK
8 TO 9 HOURS

4-pound boneless beef bottom round roast **or** chuck pot roast

4 cloves garlic

1 tablespoon chili powder

½ teaspoon ground coriander

½ teaspoon ground cumin

2 cans (10½ ounces **each**) Campbell's® Condensed Beef Broth

2 large onions, sliced (about 2 cups)

1 can (about 15 ounces) whole peeled tomatoes

1 can (about 15 ounces) red kidney beans, rinsed and drained

¾ cup **uncooked** regular long-grain white rice

1. Cut **4** evenly-spaced slits in the beef. Insert **1** garlic clove into each slit. Mix the chili powder, coriander and cumin in a small bowl. Rub the chili powder mixture over the beef. Place the beef into a 6-quart slow cooker.

2. Mix the broth, onions, tomatoes, beans and rice in a medium bowl. Pour over the beef.

3. Cover and cook on LOW for 8 to 9 hours* or until the beef is fork-tender.

Or on HIGH for 4 to 5 hours.

Swiss Steak Delight

MAKES 6 SERVINGS

$1\frac{1}{2}$	pounds boneless beef round steak, cut into 6 pieces
$\frac{1}{2}$	pound new potatoes, cut into quarters
$1\frac{1}{2}$	cups fresh **or** frozen whole baby carrots
1	medium onion, sliced (about $\frac{1}{2}$ cup)
1	can (about $14\frac{1}{2}$ ounces) diced tomatoes with Italian herbs
1	can ($14\frac{1}{2}$ ounces) Campbell's® Beef Gravy

PREP
15 MINUTES

COOK
8 TO 9 HOURS,
10 MINUTES

1. Cook the beef in 2 batches in a 12-inch nonstick skillet over medium-high heat until it's well browned.

2. Place the potatoes, carrots, onion and beef into a $3\frac{1}{2}$-quart slow cooker. Stir the tomatoes and gravy in a medium bowl. Pour over the beef and vegetables.

3. Cover and cook on LOW for 8 to 9 hours* or until the beef is fork-tender.

*Or on HIGH for 4 to 5 hours.

Bratwurst with Creamy Apple and Onion Compote

MAKES 8 SERVINGS

PREP
15 MINUTES

COOK
4 TO 5 HOURS

2 large red onions, thinly sliced (about 2 cups)

2 pounds bratwurst

2 cans (10¾ ounces **each**) Campbell's® Condensed Cream of Celery Soup (Regular **or** 98% Fat Free)

1 can (12 ounces) beer

8 ounces fresh whole baby carrots

1 tablespoon Dijon-style mustard

2 medium apples, cored and cut into quarters

Hot egg noodles **or** mashed potatoes

Chopped parsley (optional)

1. Stir the onions, bratwurst, soup, beer, carrots, mustard and apples in a 6-quart slow cooker.

2. Cover and cook on HIGH for 4 to 5 hours or until the onions are tender. Serve with the noodles. Sprinkle with the parsley, if desired.

Kielbasa with Apples, Onions and Sauerkraut

MAKES 8 SERVINGS

2 pounds kielbasa (beef or turkey), cut into 2-inch-long pieces

1 package (16 ounces) prepared sauerkraut, drained

2 cans (10¾ ounces **each**) Campbell's® Condensed French Onion Soup

3 medium apples, cored and cut into quarters

1 cup water **or** white wine

2 tablespoons Dijon-style mustard

1. Stir the kielbasa, sauerkraut, soup, apples, water and mustard in a 6-quart slow cooker.

2. Cover and cook on HIGH for 4 to 5 hours or until the apples are tender.

PREP
10 MINUTES

COOK
4 TO 5 HOURS

Campbell's Kitchen Tip

This dish is delicious served over hot mashed potatoes or egg noodles.

Tuscan Beef Stew

MAKES 8 SERVINGS

PREP
15 MINUTES

COOK
8 TO 9 HOURS,
10 MINUTES

1 can (10¾ ounces) Campbell's® Condensed Tomato Soup

1 can (10½ ounces) Campbell's® Condensed Beef Broth

½ cup Burgundy wine **or** other dry red wine or water

1 teaspoon dried Italian seasoning, crushed

½ teaspoon garlic powder

1 can (about 14½ ounces) diced tomatoes with Italian herbs

3 large carrots, cut into 1-inch pieces (about 2 cups)

2 pounds beef for stew, cut into 1-inch pieces

2 cans (about 16 ounces **each**) white kidney beans (cannellini), rinsed and drained

1. Stir the soup, broth, wine, Italian seasoning, garlic powder, tomatoes, carrots and beef in a 3½-quart slow cooker.

2. Cover and cook on LOW for 8 to 9 hours* or until the beef is fork-tender.

3. Stir in the beans. Turn the heat to HIGH. Cook for 10 minutes or until the mixture is hot.

Or on HIGH for 4 to 5 hours.

Quick-Prep Desserts

Chocolate Cappuccino Bread Pudding

MAKES 8 CUPS

PREP
20 MINUTES

COOK
2 TO 3 HOURS

Vegetable cooking spray

1 loaf (24 ounces) Pepperidge Farm® Farmhouse Hearty White Bread, cut into cubes (about 15 cups)

4 cups milk

¼ cup heavy cream

6 large eggs

1 tablespoon vanilla extract

1 cup granulated sugar

1 cup packed light brown sugar

¼ cup unsweetened cocoa powder

1 tablespoon instant espresso powder

1 cup semi-sweet chocolate pieces

Campbell's Kitchen Tip

*Serve warm with whipped cream **or** vanilla ice cream and topped with toasted chopped almonds **or** pecans.*

1. Spray the inside of a 6-quart slow cooker with the cooking spray. Place the bread cubes into the cooker.

2. Beat the milk, cream, eggs and vanilla with a fork in a large bowl.

3. Stir the granulated sugar, brown sugar, cocoa powder and espresso powder in a medium bowl. Stir into the milk mixture.

4. Pour the milk mixture over the bread cubes. Stir and press the bread cubes into the milk mixture to coat. Sprinkle with the chocolate pieces.

5. Cover and cook on HIGH for 2 to 3 hours or until set.

Peach & Berry Cobbler

MAKES 6 CUPS

PREP
5 MINUTES

COOK
4 TO 5 HOURS

Vegetable cooking spray
1 package (16 ounces) frozen peach slices
1 package (16 ounces) frozen mixed berries (strawberries, blueberries and raspberries)
1 cup V8 V-Fusion® Peach Mango juice
1 tablespoon cornstarch
1 teaspoon almond extract
1 package (18.25 ounces) yellow cake mix
1 stick butter (4 ounces), cut into pieces
Confectioners' sugar

1. Spray the inside of a 6-quart slow cooker with the cooking spray. Place the peaches and berries into the cooker.

2. Stir the V8, cornstarch and almond extract in a small bowl. Pour into the cooker.

3. Sprinkle the cake mix over the fruit mixture. Dot with the butter.

4. Layer **8** pieces of paper towel across the top of the cooker. Place the cooker cover on top*.

5. Cook on LOW for 4 to 5 hours** or until the fruit mixture boils and thickens and the topping is cooked though. Sprinkle with the confectioners' sugar.

*The paper towels will absorb any moisture that rises to the top of the cooker.

**Do not lift the cover on the cooker at all during the first 3 hours of the cook time.

Tropical Pudding Cake

MAKES 8 SERVINGS

PREP
10 MINUTES

COOK
2 TO 3 HOURS,
5 MINUTES

STAND
30 MINUTES

2 cups all-purpose flour
$\frac{2}{3}$ cup sugar
2 teaspoons baking powder
1 teaspoon ground cinnamon
8 tablespoons butter, melted
1 cup milk
1 can (21 ounces) canned sliced apples
1 can (20 ounces) crushed pineapple, drained
$\frac{3}{4}$ cup toasted walnuts
2 cups packed brown sugar
2 cups V8 Splash® Tropical Blend
2 cups water
   Vanilla ice cream (optional)

1. Stir the flour, sugar, baking powder and cinnamon in a large bowl. Stir **half** of the butter and the milk into the flour mixture. Stir the apples, pineapple and walnuts into the batter. Pour into a 4-quart slow cooker.

2. Heat the brown sugar, V8, water and remaining butter in a 3-quart saucepan over medium-high heat to a boil. Cook for 2 minutes, stirring often. Pour over the batter in the slow cooker.

3. Cover and cook on HIGH for 2 to 3 hours or until a toothpick inserted in the center comes out with moist crumbs.

4. Turn off the cooker. Uncover and let stand for 30 minutes. Serve with vanilla ice cream, if desired.

Triple Chocolate Pudding Cake with Raspberry Sauce

MAKES 12 SERVINGS

PREP
10 MINUTES

COOK
6 TO 7 HOURS

Vegetable cooking spray
1 package (18½ ounces) chocolate cake mix
1 package (about 3.9 ounces) chocolate instant pudding and pie filling mix
2 cups sour cream
4 eggs
1 cup V8® 100% Vegetable Juice
¾ cup vegetable oil
1 cup semi-sweet chocolate pieces
Raspberry dessert topping
Whipped cream

1. Spray the inside of a 3½- to 4-quart slow cooker with the cooking spray.

2. Place the cake mix, pudding mix, sour cream, eggs, V8 and oil in a large bowl. Beat with an electric mixer on medium speed for 2 minutes. Stir in the chocolate pieces. Pour the batter into the cooker.

3. Cover and cook on LOW for 6 to 7 hours or until a toothpick inserted in the center comes out with moist crumbs. Serve with the raspberry topping and whipped cream.

Gingerbread with Dried Cherries

MAKES 6 SERVINGS

PREP
15 MINUTES

COOK
2 TO 3 HOURS

Vegetable cooking spray
3 cups all-purpose flour
1 teaspoon baking powder
1 teaspoon baking soda
1 teaspoon ground cinnamon
1 teaspoon ground ginger
¼ teaspoon salt
¼ teaspoon allspice
1 cup butter, softened
½ cup packed brown sugar
4 eggs
¾ cup molasses
1 cup V8® 100% Vegetable Juice
1 cup dried cherries
Whipped cream (optional)

1. Spray a 4-quart slow cooker with the cooking spray.

2. Stir the flour, baking powder, baking soda, cinnamon, ginger, salt and allspice in a medium bowl.

3. Place the butter and brown sugar into a large bowl. Beat with an electric mixer on medium speed until it's creamy. Beat in the eggs and molasses. Alternately stir in the flour mixture with the V8. Stir in the cherries. Pour the batter into the cooker.

4. Cover and cook on for HIGH for 2 to 3 hours or until a toothpick inserted in the center comes out with moist crumbs. Spoon the gingerbread into bowls. Top with the whipped cream, if desired.

Apple Cherry Pastries with Vanilla Cream

MAKES 12 PASTRIES

PREP
15 MINUTES

COOK
4 TO 5 HOURS

- 8 apples (about 3 pounds), peeled and cut into $\frac{1}{4}$-inch slices
- $\frac{1}{2}$ cup dried cherries
- 1 cup sugar
- $\frac{1}{2}$ teaspoon grated lemon peel
- 2 packages (10 ounces **each**) Pepperidge Farm® Puff Pastry Shells
- 1 package (3.4 ounces) vanilla instant pudding and pie filling mix
- 3 cups milk

1. Stir the apples, cherries, sugar and lemon peel in a 4-quart slow cooker.

2. Cover and cook on LOW for 4 to 5 hours or until the apples are tender.

3. Prepare the pastry shells according to the package directions. Let cool.

4. Beat the pudding mix and milk in a medium bowl with a whisk for about 2 minutes or until it thickens.

5. Divide the apple mixture among the pastry shells. Spoon the pudding mixture over the apple mixture.

Harvest Fruit Compote

MAKES 5 CUPS

PREP
10 MINUTES

COOK
4 TO 5 HOURS

Campbell's Kitchen Tip

The compote can be served warm or cold. Try it warm spooned over vanilla ice cream or pound cake. Try it warm or cold as an accompaniment to roast pork loin.

2 packages (12 ounces **each**) prunes (about 4 cups)

1 package (7 ounces) mixed dried fruit (about 1½ cups)

1 package (7 ounces) dried apricots (about 1½ cups)

½ cup dried cranberries

⅓ cup raisins

4 cups V8 V-Fusion® Pomegranate Blueberry juice

1 cup white Zinfandel wine

1 teaspoon grated lemon peel

1 teaspoon vanilla extract

1. Stir the prunes, mixed fruit, apricots, cranberries, raisins, V8, wine, lemon peel and vanilla in a 4- to 6-quart slow cooker.

2. Cover and cook on HIGH for 4 to 5 hours*.

Or on LOW for 7 to 8 hours.

Blueberry Compote with Lemon Dumplings

MAKES 8 SERVINGS

PREP
5 MINUTES

COOK
3 TO 4 HOURS,
20 MINUTES

2 pounds frozen blueberries
¾ cup sugar
1 cup V8 V-Fusion® Pomegranate Blueberry juice
2 cups buttermilk baking mix
⅔ cup milk
1 tablespoon grated lemon peel
Vanilla ice cream (optional)

1. Stir the blueberries, ½ **cup** of the sugar and the V8 in a 4-quart slow cooker.

2. Cover and cook on LOW for 3 to 4 hours or until the mixture boils.

3. Stir the baking mix, remaining sugar, milk and lemon peel in a small bowl. Drop the batter by rounded tablespoonsful over the blueberry mixture.

4. Cover and cook on HIGH for 20 to 25 minutes or until the dumplings are cooked in the center. Serve with the vanilla ice cream, if desired.

Chocolate Almond Bread Pudding with Dried Cherries

MAKES 6 SERVINGS

PREP
10 MINUTES

COOK
2½ TO 3 HOURS

Vegetable cooking spray

10 slices Pepperidge Farm® White Sandwich Bread, cut into cubes (about 5 cups)

½ cup dried cherries, chopped

½ cup semi-sweet chocolate pieces

1¾ cups milk

½ cup sugar

⅓ cup unsweetened cocoa powder

½ teaspoon almond **or** vanilla extract

4 eggs, beaten

Sweetened whipped cream (optional)

Toasted almonds (optional)

1. Spray the inside of a 4½- to 5-quart slow cooker with the cooking spray.

2. Place the bread cubes into the cooker. Sprinkle with the cherries and chocolate.

3. Beat the milk, sugar, cocoa, almond extract and eggs with a fork in a medium bowl. Pour over the bread mixture. Stir and press the bread cubes into the milk mixture to coat.

4. Cover and cook on LOW for 2½ to 3 hours or until set. Serve warm with whipped cream and almonds, if desired.

Chocolate and Coconut Cream Fondue

MAKES 3 CUPS

PREP
5 MINUTES

COOK
10 MINUTES

Campbell's Kitchen Tip

Any remaining fondue can be used as an ice cream or dessert topping. Cover and refrigerate in an airtight container. Reheat in a saucepan until warm.

1 can (15 ounces) cream of coconut

2 tablespoons rum **or** 1 teaspoon rum extract (optional)

1 package (12 ounces) semi-sweet chocolate pieces

1. Stir the cream of coconut, rum and chocolate in a 2-quart saucepan. Heat over medium heat until the chocolate melts, stirring occasionally.

2. Pour the chocolate mixture into a slow cooker or fondue pot. Serve warm with dippers.

Serve with some or all of these dippers: Assorted Pepperidge Farm® Cookies, Pepperidge Farm® Graham Giant Goldfish® Baked Snack Crackers, whole strawberries, banana chunks, dried pineapple pieces and fresh pineapple chunks.

Brown Sugar Spice Cake

MAKES 8 SERVINGS

Vegetable cooking spray
1 can (10¾ ounces) Campbell's® Condensed
    Tomato Soup
½ cup water
2 eggs
1 box (about 18 ounces) spice cake mix
1¼ cups hot water
¾ cup packed brown sugar
1 teaspoon ground cinnamon
Vanilla ice cream

PREP
10 MINUTES

COOK
2 TO 2½ HOURS

1. Spray the inside of a 3½- to 4-quart slow cooker with the cooking spray.

2. Mix the soup, water, eggs and cake mix in a medium bowl according to the package directions. Pour into the cooker.

3. Mix the water, brown sugar and cinnamon in a small bowl. Pour over the batter.

4. Cover and cook on HIGH for 2 to 2½ hours or until a toothpick inserted in the center comes out clean.

5. Spoon the cake into bowls, spooning the sauce from the bottom of the cooker. Serve warm with the ice cream.

Not Your Gramma's Kugel

MAKES 6 SERVINGS

PREP
10 MINUTES

COOK
2 TO 2½ HOURS

Vegetable cooking spray
1 package (12 ounces) **uncooked** medium egg noodles
½ cup currants
1 can (10¾ ounces) Campbell's® Condensed Cheddar Cheese Soup
1 cup small curd cottage cheese
¾ cup sugar
1 teaspoon grated orange peel
2 eggs, beaten

1. Spray the inside of a 3½-quart slow cooker with the cooking spray.

2. Cook the noodles according to the package directions until almost done. Drain and place in the cooker. Sprinkle with the currants.

3. Beat the soup, cottage cheese, sugar, orange peel and eggs with a fork in a medium bowl. Pour over the noodles. Stir to coat.

4. Cover and cook on LOW for 2 to 2½ hours or until set. Serve warm.

Raisin Cinnamon Bread Pudding

MAKES 6 SERVINGS

Vegetable cooking spray

10 slices Pepperidge Farm® Raisin Cinnamon Swirl
Bread, cut into cubes (about 5 cups)

1 can (14 ounces) sweetened condensed milk

1 cup water

1 teaspoon vanilla extract

4 eggs, beaten

Ice cream (optional)

PREP
10 MINUTES

COOK
2½ TO 3 HOURS

1. Spray the inside of a 4½- to 5-quart slow cooker with the cooking spray.

2. Place the bread cubes into the cooker.

3. Beat the milk, water, vanilla and eggs with a fork in a medium bowl. Pour over the bread mixture. Stir and press the bread cubes into the milk mixture to coat.

4. Cover and cook on LOW for 2½ to 3 hours or until set. Serve warm with the ice cream, if desired.

Mulled Pomegranate Wine

MAKES 8 CUPS

PREP
5 MINUTES

COOK
2 TO 3 HOURS

1 bottle (750 milliliters) white Cabernet **or** white Zinfandel wine

4 cups V8 V-Fusion® Pomegranate Blueberry juice

¾ cup sugar

2 cinnamon sticks

½ cup pomegranate seeds (optional)

1. Stir the wine, V8, sugar, cinnamon sticks and pomegranate seeds in a 4-quart slow cooker.

2. Cover and cook on HIGH for 2 to 3 hours or until the mixture is hot. Serve warm.

Hot Toddy

MAKES 13 SERVINGS

PREP
5 MINUTES

COOK
1 TO 2 HOURS

1 orange

15 to 20 whole cloves

2 bottles (46 ounces **each**) V8 V-Fusion® Tropical Orange juice

2 cups spiced rum

3 cinnamon sticks

2 pieces crystallized ginger root
   Cinnamon sticks (optional)

1. Stud the orange with the cloves and cut it into thick slices crosswise. Stir the orange slices, V8, rum, cinnamon sticks and ginger in a 6-quart slow cooker.

2. Cover and cook on HIGH for 1 to 2 hours or until the mixture is hot. Serve warm. Garnish each serving with an additional cinnamon stick, if desired.

Creamy Orange Rice Pudding

MAKES 8 SERVINGS

Vegetable cooking spray

4 cups V8 V-Fusion® Tropical Orange juice

½ cup **uncooked** regular long-grain white rice

½ cup dried cranberries **or** golden raisins

1½ cups heavy cream

¼ teaspoon ground cinnamon

PREP
5 MINUTES

COOK
4 TO 5 HOURS

STAND
10 MINUTES

1. Spray the inside of a 6-quart slow cooker with the cooking spray. Stir the V8, rice and cranberries in the cooker.

2. Cover and cook on HIGH for 4 to 5 hours or until the rice is tender, stirring once during cooking.

3. Stir the cream into the cooker. Pour the rice mixture into a 2-quart serving bowl. Let stand for 10 minutes. Sprinkle with the cinnamon before serving. Serve warm or cover and refrigerate until ready to serve.

Campbell's Kitchen Tip

The pudding will thicken upon standing.

Index

Desserts

Metric Conversion Chart

VOLUME MEASUREMENTS (dry)

$1/8$ teaspoon = 0.5 mL
$1/4$ teaspoon = 1 mL
$1/2$ teaspoon = 2 mL
$3/4$ teaspoon = 4 mL
1 teaspoon = 5 mL
1 tablespoon = 15 mL
2 tablespoons = 30 mL
$1/4$ cup = 60 mL
$1/3$ cup = 75 mL
$1/2$ cup = 125 mL
$2/3$ cup = 150 mL
$3/4$ cup = 175 mL
1 cup = 250 mL
2 cups = 1 pint = 500 mL
3 cups = 750 mL
4 cups = 1 quart = 1 L

VOLUME MEASUREMENTS (fluid)

1 fluid ounce (2 tablespoons) = 30 mL
4 fluid ounces ($1/2$ cup) = 125 mL
8 fluid ounces (1 cup) = 250 mL
12 fluid ounces ($1 1/2$ cups) = 375 mL
16 fluid ounces (2 cups) = 500 mL

WEIGHTS (mass)

$1/2$ ounce = 15 g
1 ounce = 30 g
3 ounces = 90 g
4 ounces = 120 g
8 ounces = 225 g
10 ounces = 285 g
12 ounces = 360 g
16 ounces = 1 pound = 450 g

DIMENSIONS

$1/16$ inch = 2 mm
$1/8$ inch = 3 mm
$1/4$ inch = 6 mm
$1/2$ inch = 1.5 cm
$3/4$ inch = 2 cm
1 inch = 2.5 cm

OVEN TEMPERATURES

250°F = 120°C
275°F = 140°C
300°F = 150°C
325°F = 160°C
350°F = 180°C
375°F = 190°C
400°F = 200°C
425°F = 220°C
450°F = 230°C

BAKING PAN AND DISH EQUIVALENTS

Utensil	Size in Inches	Size in Centimeters	Volume	Metric Volume
Baking or Cake Pan (square or rectangular)	8×8×2	20×20×5	8 cups	2 L
	9×9×2	23×23×5	10 cups	2.5 L
	13×9×2	33×23×5	12 cups	3 L
Loaf Pan	8½×4½×2½	21×11×6	6 cups	1.5 L
	9×9×3	23×13×7	8 cups	2 L
Round Layer Cake Pan	8×1½	20×4	4 cups	1 L
	9×1½	23×4	5 cups	1.25 L
Pie Plate	8×1½	20×4	4 cups	1 L
	9×1½	23×4	5 cups	1.25 L
Baking Dish or Casserole			1 quart/4 cups	1 L
			1½ quart/6 cups	1.5 L
			2 quart/8 cups	2 L
			3 quart/12 cups	3 L